Country Lawyers

Country Lawyers

THE IMPACT OF CONTEXT ON PROFESSIONAL PRACTICE

Donald D. Landon

Foreword by
John P. Heinz

PRAEGER

New York
Westport, Connecticut
London

Copyright Acknowledgments

Tables 2.1–2.7, 5.1–5.3, 7.1, 7.4–7.6 are taken from *Chicago Lawyers: The Social Structure of the Bar* by John P. Heinz and Edward O. Laumann. © The Russell Sage Foundation, 1982. Used with permission of the Russell Sage Foundation.

An earlier version of Chapter 8 appeared as "Clients, Colleagues, and Community: The Shaping of Zealous Advocacy in Country Law Practice" in the *American Bar Foundation Research Journal*, 1985, 1, 81–111 and is reprinted here in revised form with permission of the American Bar Foundation and the *ABF Research Journal*.

Library of Congress Cataloging-in-Publication Data

Landon, Donald D., 1930–
Country lawyers : the impact of context on professional practice / Donald D. Landon.
p. cm.
Includes bibliographical references.
ISBN 0–275–93042–4 (alk. paper)
1. Country lawyers—United States. 2. Practice of law—United States. I. Title.
KF297.L355 1990
340'.023'73—dc20 89–16220

Library of Congress Catalog Card Number: 89–16220
ISBN: 0–275–93042–4

First published in 1990

Praeger Publishers, One Madison Avenue, New York, NY 10010
A division of Greenwood Press, Inc.

Printed in the United States of America

The paper used in this book complies with the Permanent Paper Standard issued by the National Information Standards Organization (Z39.48–1984).

P

In order to keep this title in print and available to the academic community, this edition was produced using digital reprint technology in a relatively short print run. This would not have been attainable using traditional methods. Although the cover has been changed from its original appearance, the text remains the same and all materials and methods used still conform to the highest book-making standards.

To L
with l

CONTENTS

TABLES

FOREWORD

Long before I began to do research on the social structure of the Chicago bar, I was an observer of the legal profession in a small town. My family was not engaged in the law business, but like most other residents of towns of 5,000 we found a good share of our entertainment in accounts of the doings at the courthouse. As topics of conversation, the exploits of lawyers and the folly of their clients had serious competition only from speculation on the amount and timing of past rain, learned commentary on the performance of the high school basketball team, and discussions of the myriad interrelationships among the old families in town. (At our dining table, accounts of who begat whom were given as much attention as they are in the Old Testament or in explanations of the job qualifications of Chicago officeholders.) I lived then in Carlinville, Illinois, the county seat of Macoupin County, about 250 miles south of Chicago.

The story of the building of the courthouse, itself, was an important part of the legal lore of the community, even though it had been built nearly a century before my time there. A version of the story is included in a standard work on Illinois architecture (Koeper, 1968, 32):

> The history of the building of this courthouse is a notorious one, centering on its cost, which plunged the county into debt for forty-three years. Originally a sum of $50,000 was voted, but the completed work ran to $1,380,000 (in 1868 dollars!). The courthouse came into existence only after long litigation and heated opposition. The four commissioners in charge, assisted by Governor John M. Palmer, himself a Macoupin County resident, ultimately triumphed over the anti-courthouse party who tried to stop the work

and challenged the legality of the ever-increasing bond issues. Funds were undoubtedly mismanaged, for the building cost exactly twice its worth.

Don Landon's research on country lawyers does not deal in such sordid tales of misuse of public monies. He leaves that to the daily news reports from Washington. Instead, Landon gives us the most systematic and thorough analysis that we have yet had of the sociology of the rural bar.

More than two decades ago, Joel Handler wrote an excellent book about the bar in a city of 90,000, which he called "Prairie City" (Handler, 1967). Landon includes comparative data about a similar moderate-sized city, Springfield, Missouri, but he is primarily concerned with lawyers who work in smaller places. He gives us unique findings about their work, about the ways in which they strive to establish a successful practice and to attain prestige, about the extent of their independence or autonomy, and, above all, about their relationships with their communities.

This book includes a number of comparisons of the findings concerning rural lawyers to the data that Ed Laumann and I collected on Chicago lawyers about eight years earlier, as well as to Landon's own data on Springfield lawyers. This permits Landon to locate the rural lawyers within a broader social and professional context. His comparison of the country lawyers to the segment of the Chicago bar that deals with "personal plight" cases is especially enlightening.

While Laumann and I argued that the social structure of the Chicago bar was "client driven," Landon finds that the country lawyers are "community driven." What the two bars have in common is that neither is "lawyer driven." Both respond to social forces that are external to the profession, and neither appears to be greatly governed by professional norms. The ethnoreligious and political diversity that we found to be important ingredients of the structure of the Chicago bar, though strongly associated with client differences there, were of course also "community" influences. Landon concludes: "The difference is, in the rural case, the containing community is more homogeneous, which produces a mirroring homogeneity in the profession."

The rural lawyers interviewed by Landon reveal in many ways their intimate ties to their communities. The ties, in fact, are so strong that they impose severe constraints on the professional judgment or freedom of action of the country practitioners. One of the lawyers told Landon that his decision to accept a malpractice case against a local doctor may have "finished" his practice in the community, another told him that he would "never take on a sexual abuse case in this town," and another that filing a civil rights suit against the local school district was "the worst mistake of my career" and was "held against me for ten years." Obviously, such statements have implications for the availability of local counsel in controversial cases. Those lawyers are not likely to make the same mistakes again.

But the close ties of these lawyers to the residents of their communities have a more positive, caring side as well. Landon tells us that country lawyers are consulted about decisions on whether to buy a car for a 17-year-old son, whether to place an elderly parent in a nursing home, and whether there is a market in the community for another dress shop. These lawyers are truly the friends and neighbors of their clients, and they are involved in their clients' lives in ways that would be impossible and unimaginable for most Chicago lawyers.

Landon's comparison of the structures of intra-professional prestige in Chicago and in rural Missouri reflects these differences. One of the more surprising findings of the Chicago study was that the distribution of status among the legal specialists or fields of law practice was not significantly determined by the earnings of the practitioners in the field. Rather, Laumann and I argued, prestige was determined largely by the power or social standing of the clients—the more powerful the clients of the area of practice, the more prestigious it was within the profession. Landon finds a very different picture in rural Missouri. Lacking the degree of client differentiation that exists in Chicago, intra-professional prestige in the country context appears to be determined primarily by the income potential of the field of practice. Thus, the kinds of legal work that produce greater wealth for lawyers are accorded higher status within the profession (as we had thought they might be in Chicago).

The potential for producing lawyer income is not always associated with the power or standing of clients. One of the most striking examples of this is that in the rural context the prestige of "negligence" (or "personal injury") work on behalf of plaintiffs is ranked substantially higher than that done for the defendants in such cases, which usually means work done for insurance companies. In Chicago, the opposite is true. In fact, in Chicago the side of a field of law that represents the more powerful clients was consistently accorded higher prestige than the side that represents less powerful clients. Not in rural Missouri! Though their political and social values are relatively conservative, rural lawyers appear to feel a greater degree of sympathy for and identification with the underdog. These lawyers actually *know* some underdogs; they live in close proximity to them; not in Lake Forest or Winnetka.

To one who grew up in Carlinville and has since spent some fair amount of time in the company of lawyers, this all rings very true. Indeed, some of the truths have a timeless quality. To confirm this, I have consulted the chapter on the bench and bar in my copy of the 1879 history of Macoupin County. It includes this description of the career of an early Carlinville lawyer, one John A. Chesnut (Anon., 1879, 53):

> He had a common-school education, and a fair knowledge of Latin. After reading diligently, such elementary works on law as were in his preceptor's library, at the December term of the Supreme Court, in 1837, he was admitted to the bar. He soon gained a fair share of the legal business of this county, and extended his business into adjoining counties. After John M. Palmer, Esq., came into the profession, he and Mr. Chesnut, for a good many years, divided a large part of the business between them. They found hard work, but pay was small, and they, like most of the lawyers of the day, prompted

by ambition, engaged a little in politics and from a love of lucre sought office. To what pitch of eminence Mr. Chesnut might have attained in his profession, had he not left it in 1855 to engage in other lucrative pursuits, can never be known. He became wealthy, but the disasters to business occurring in 1873, and again in 1878, swept away his accumulations, and he is now entering anew upon his profession at Springfield.

John A. Chesnut would not be far out-of-place in Don Landon's sample. Landon's country lawyers, like Chesnut, are entrepreneurs—they are active in a broad mix of business ventures as well as in the practice of law (indeed, the law practice may be regarded as only another of those business ventures)—and, again like Chesnut, they dabble in politics, often seek public office, and generally display a "love of lucre." It is good to know that there are some constants.

John P. Heinz
Distinguished Research Fellow
American Bar Foundation
Owen L. Coon Professor of Law
Northwestern University

PREFACE

This book is about a special segment of the legal profession—lawyers practicing in the smallest settings in the United States. In Barbara Curran's (1985:243) monumental *Lawyer's Statistical Report*, more than half a million attorneys practicing in the United States are reported to be disproportionately concentrated in Standard Metropolitan Statistical Areas (SMSAs) which are defined as cities with 50,000 or more inhabitants. Eighty-eight percent of the practicing bar are located in these metropolitan settings. The remaining 12 percent (63,515) are practicing in smaller settings ranging from county seats with as few as 256 residents to principal cities of under 50,000.

For obvious reasons, the metropolitan bar has been most thoroughly examined by scholars. The shakers and movers of the profession are located in big cities. The clients of national consequence are more typically located in metropolitan settings. The law schools and the universities from which the studies are done are, by and large, urban institutions and they respond to their milieu.

Sheer curiosity about what law practice is like away from urban specialization and elite clients may itself justify a study of the nonmetropolitan bar. But there are more substantial reasons why this study was undertaken. The evidence has been building that the legal profession is a highly fragmented professional community. John Heinz and Edward Laumann's (1982) profound study of the Chicago bar found attorneys living in different worlds, practicing with such different clients, colleagues, and concerns as to bifurcate the profession into at least two separate hemispheres. This multiplicity of professions within a single professional category appears to reflect the diversity of the metropolitan setting. It suggests that the legal profession is profoundly structured by the context in which it practices. Rather than being shaped by the internal logic of legal doctrine or fields of practice, the bar appears to be shaped by external forces including the social, economic, and political structure of the containing community.

This sensitivity to external forces was detected by Heinz and Laumann who characterized the bar as an "overdetermined social system" (Heinz and Laumann, 1982:69). Presumably, the hallmark of professional practice is its autonomy, its independence from external constraints. The Chicago study documents that this presumed independence is more apparent than real.

If the practicing bar is profoundly shaped by the metropolitan environment, as virtually all studies indicate, is it also shaped by more modest settings? If the powerful metropolitan dynamics of ethnicity, socioeconomic diversity, and client contrast (which range from corporations whose revenues exceed the GNP of entire countries to individuals who possess little more than their personal plights) have a profound shaping effect on the social structure of the metropolitan bar, is there any equivalent shaping done in small-scale settings? In short, is there an ecology of law practice; and if so, what are the salient factors that shape the practice characteristics of attorneys in small settings?

This study of the rural bar is unique in the sense that it is the first broad-based study of small-scale settings. Because the data gathered was, in many instances, identical to the data gathered in Heinz and Laumann's Chicago study, it enables comparison. Moreover, we also gathered data from a middle-size city (150,000), which enabled a more systematic comparison of the changes that occur as one moves from the smallest community through a middle-size urban setting to the massive metropolitan setting. The rural data presented in this study enable that more sweeping analysis to be done for the first time.

The study had its beginnings in a conversation with Spencer L. Kimball in the fall of 1981. Kimball was executive director of the American Bar Foundation (ABF) in Chicago at the time. I had just completed an exploratory study of the impact of the rural environment on professionalism (Landon, 1982). At that time Jack Heinz and Ed Laumann were finishing their work on the Chicago bar study, and Kimball suggested that a more extensive study of the nonmetropolitan bar would be an excellent addition to the work currently being completed on the Chicago bar.

A proposal was prepared and the American Bar Foundation invited me to come to Chicago as a visiting scholar for the 1982–83 academic year to undertake the study with their support. It was actually March of 1983 before I arrived in Chicago. From June 1982 through February 1983 I traveled throughout the state of Missouri interviewing 201 attorneys practicing in 94 counties and 116 different communities. From March through August 1983 I coded the data, deciphered hundreds of pages of field notes, and began the analysis.

Earlier, in 1982, two associates helped in gathering the data from the middle-size city, Springfield, Missouri. Micki A. Pulley and Julie Williams interviewed 77 Springfield attorneys using the same interview schedule I was using in the outstate communities.

This study focuses on the smallest practice settings and thus tries to capture the structuring influences that operate in intimate environments. Of the 201 interviews, 62 were done in towns of 2,500 or less. Fifty were done in towns of between 2,500 and 5,000. Another 51 were done in towns of between 5,000 and 10,000. Thirty-eight were done in small cities of between 10,000 and 20,000.

The Missouri Bar under the leadership of its then executive director, Wade Baker, gave exceptional support throughout the entire study. Following Baker's retirement, Keith Birkes, the new executive director, continued the support through the completion of the project. The acknowledgments extend to the 201 attorneys in small places and the 77 in Springfield who graciously agreed to share their time, facts, and insights about their work, and their goodwill when some of the interviews exceeded the hour and a half planned for them.

A number of people at the American Bar Foundation contributed significantly to the study. Jack Heinz, executive director of the ABF during my visiting scholar appointment there, sharpened my insights through numerous conversations including his own memories of the small town where he grew up, Carlinville, Illinois. Barbara Curran's steady inquiries—''How are things going?''—gave me an opportunity to share tentative insights and test them against work she was currently doing on the lawyer statistical report. Bob Nelson facilitated the first discussion with Spencer Kimball about doing the study and then continued to lend moral support during the long periods of coding and organizing field notes. Marcie Patton provided technical assistance in getting the data on computer and cleaning it so that analysis could proceed. Bette Sikes, Tom Davies, and Terrence Halliday gave valuable help as the first article for the *American Bar Foundation Research Journal* took shape.

Readying the manuscript for publication was the special contribution of Avon Bradshaw, secretary to the department of sociology, anthropology, and social work at Southwest Missouri State University in Springfield.

The current study can best be described as a beginning effort to understand the contextual forces shaping the work of lawyers. It carries the mark of the sociologists: a probing beneath the official version of how things work. If it has successfully penetrated the facade and stimulates more systematic work on important issues, the effort will have been well rewarded.

Country Lawyers

1

THE SIGNIFICANCE OF THE RURAL SETTING FOR THE PRACTICE OF LAW

A century ago nearly every lawyer was a country lawyer. The majority of the U.S. population lived in small towns or the countryside. The powerful impact of immense corporations and metropolitan settings was yet to be felt. Most legal problems still revolved around personal businesses or the property and the plights of individuals. The law firm was still the exception and the individual practitioner still the rule.

William English captured the essence of nineteenth century law practice in Missouri. Practitioners then were

> country lawyers in every sense of the word. They had small offices on the square or sometimes in their homes, which were the meeting places for politicians, businessmen, farmers, and visiting attorneys. With the possible exception of the doctor, the lawyer knew more about the affairs of his neighbors than anyone. The rich and the poor came to him with their troubles and sought his aid and his advice. He was the counsellor of his neighbors in many personal and petty matters, as well as in their more important business relationships. (English 1947:100)

W. L. D. Jewett (1898:54, 59) recalls the inauspicious beginnings of James Carr's practice in Monroe County, Missouri, about 1850. After teaching school there for some years and mastering a Virginia accent that covered his Pennsylvania origins (since local feeling still ran high against Yankees), Carr read law and then set up shop in Paris, Missouri. His office was a small 14-by-14 room for which he could not afford a table. Consequently, "he put a board on the arm of a 'split-bottom' rocking chair'' on which he did his studying and writing. Carr's peers considered him a reasonably learned man, but no great shakes in the courtroom. Apparently he was not ''a good judge of human behavior'' and found it difficult ''to compete with the average country lawyer''—who, if nothing else, had eloquent courtroom oratory. But Carr had an eye on the horizon. He studied corporation law and at the end of the Civil War went to work for the Hannibal and St. Joe Railroad. He moved to Hannibal and then to St. Louis where he practiced corporate law, died late in the century, and ''left a good estate for his family.''

Carr's migration to the city took him where law in the twentieth century would be revolutionized. Industrialization, urbanization, and the rise of a corporate economy eclipsed law practice in small towns. Corporate clients became the focus of legal activity. These new clients reproduced their likeness in massive, departmentalized law firms with branch offices across the country and overseas. Small towns, their people, their institutions and even their lawyers became the subject of nostalgia, as in the writings of authors such as James Cozzens (1937, 1965).

Despite the romaticizing, small towns still exist in the United States. Attorneys still practice there. And the migration from rural settings to big cities has been reversed for at least a decade. But so overwhelming has been the urbanization of the United States that small town phenomena are only occasionally given serious study. Virtually all the research on the legal profession in the twentieth century has been done in metropolitan settings (Maru, 1986). Reading that literature, one is led to conclude that country lawyers have disappeared.

The fact is, rural law practice is alive and, for the most part, well. The question is, how has the urbanization and corporatization of law practice impacted the country lawyer? Is the nostalgic image of rural practice conveyed by Cozzens anything like current fact? In what ways do the practice patterns of modern country lawyers approximate those of urban attorneys? If the metropolitan environment has spawned many different professions of law—as current studies suggest (Heinz and Laumann, 1982)—does the small town environment add yet another unique dimension to an increasingly fragmented professional community? How do intimacy and law practice interface in midwestern small towns in the late twentieth century? Is the scale of the environment and the presumed intimacy of relationships in rural settings significant in shaping what lawyers do and how they do it? Is ''people practice'' in the country any different from people practice in urban settings? These were the provocative questions that sent us into the small towns of Missouri to talk to country lawyers in the last quarter of the twentieth century.

THE MEANING OF THE RURAL-URBAN CONTINUUM

So compelling and so pervasive has the shift been to an urban society, and so deeply have urban influences penetrated rural environments that the utility of the concept of "rural-urban continuum" has begun to be questioned (Bradshaw and Blakely, 1979; Taylor and Jones, 1964; Bender, 1975:185). In fact, John Friedman and John Miller (1965:312–20) yielded to the then current fad and declared that, from a sociological and indeed an economic standpoint, what is properly urban and properly rural "can no longer be distinguished." While that may be judged an extreme statement, it is true that traditional conceptions of what is rural and what is urban are changing. The concept "rural" once appeared to have a relatively singular meaning built around notions of an agricultural economy and low density settlement. Now "rural" carries a variety of meanings. As John Cornman and Barbara Kincaid point out,

> Rural includes the Green Mountains of Vermont, a ski resort in New York, a college town in Pennsylvania, a coal mining community in Kentucky, a poor town in the black belt of the South, unincorporated communities of migrant farm worker families in Texas, Indian nations in Oklahoma, family and corporate farms in the Midwest, fishing communities in Washington. (Cornman and Kincaid, 1984:2)

In addition to the multifaceted character of current rural settlements, it has also been cogently argued that the once separate and somewhat autonomous small towns are now caught up in the "massification" of U.S. society. Increasingly—goes the argument—small towns are being penetrated to the core by economic, political, and social influences emanating from the larger centers of urban power so that their uniqueness is becoming a matter of memory rather than reality (Vidich and Bensman, 1968; Martindale and Hansen, 1969).

But while the debate goes on over the loss of the distinction between rural and urban America, hundreds of thousands of Americans are pulling up stakes and moving from cities to small towns and the rural countryside to embrace what they believe to be the tangible differences between rural and urban. On balance, the evidence is that their perceptions of a difference are accurate. In rural America there is both persistence and change (Ford, 1978). There is evidence of massification to be sure. But there is also evidence of persisting qualities that have distinguished rural from urban settings for generations.

The central problem of this study is to identify what remains unique about the small context and how that shapes the conduct of law practice there. But before proceeding to that issue we must explore the question of the sensitivity and vulnerability of the legal profession to the external environment in which it practices.

THE LEGAL PROFESSION AS AN OVERDETERMINED SOCIAL SYSTEM

In an earlier seminal paper, William Goode (1957) argues that professions are unique communities distinguished by an internally consistent set of values that set them apart from their "containing communities." He argues that a profession can rightly be called "a community within a community" because: (1) its members are bound together by a sense of identity; (2) its role definition vis-à-vis both members and outsiders is shared throughout the professional ranks; (3) there is a unique and common language not fully understood by outsiders; (4) the social limits of the profession are clear; and (5) the profession reproduces itself socially through control over new trainees in professional schools.

This picture of professions as subcultures enjoying high levels of solidarity suggests that the professional community is relatively impervious to the uniqueness of a local environment.

But research into the professions has cast considerable doubt on Goode's thesis (Bucher and Strauss, 1961; Carlin, 1962, 1966; Freidson, 1972; Heinz and Laumann, 1982). The evidence is overwhelming that many of the professions are anything but communities. The growth of specialization in professional practice has clearly created a multiplicity of subgroups within such professions as medicine and law. In the case of the legal profession, Heinz and Laumann (1982) have documented that—quite contrary to Goode's argument—lawyers tend to reflect the outlook, perspectives, and values of their distinct clientele. Rather than being a distinct professional subculture impervious to the structuring effect of the environment, the legal profession appears to mirror its immediate environment and be structured by the interests of its various clientele.

The legal profession has thus been described as an "overdetermined social system" (Heinz and Laumann 1982:69). Heinz and Laumann appear to use the concept in a statistical or causal sense—meaning that there are several causes, any of which might be sufficient, that are all pushing the structure of the bar in the same direction. Thus, the inference is that the structure of the bar in Chicago is "multiply determined," or determined by more than one sufficient cause. The central finding of the Chicago study is that the bar is shaped ultimately by a variety of influences, most of which are external to the profession.

This shaping effect of the external world on the internal life of the legal profession can be illustrated by the impact of the corporation on the structure of law practice. The emergence of the public corporation essentially generated a new species of law practice; the corporate law firm. C. Wright Mills documents the affinity of large-firm law practice with the corporation that is its client.

> In fulfilling his function, the successful lawyer has created his office in the image of the corporations he has come to defend. . . . As the new business system becomes specialized with distinct sections and particular legal problems of its own, so do lawyers become experts in distinct sections and particular problems, pushing the interests of those sections rather than standing outside the business system and serving a law which coordinates the parts of society. (Mills, 1951:122)

This new entity within the legal profession functions much like a prism, "refracting social change upon the professional culture and back again to the larger society" (Auerbach, 1976:21). The priorities of the corporate clientele have shaped the priorities of "professional education, career patterns, ethics, mobility and the availability and distribution of legal services—indeed the very meaning of law and justice" (Auerbach, 1976:21). This structure effect of the external environment on the internal life of the profession has been nothing less than spectacular.

But the impact of the public environment on law practice goes beyond the bifurcation of metropolitan practice into at least two separate and unequal hemispheres of professional activity with little interaction between them (Heinz and Laumann, 1982:319). There are some identifiable characteristics of law practice that make it an overdetermined social system—a segment of social reality that is more creature than creator of events and environments.

First, the history of the profession in U.S. society is replete with evidence that law practice is a highly adaptable enterprise (Hurst, 1950:297). Contrary to the relatively focused work of the medical profession, law work is decidedly more diffuse. Geoffrey Hazard suggests that, for all the studies that have been done of law practice, the one thing we still don't know is what exactly lawyers do. Hazard describes their functions as "diverse, complex and laden." Because the "law is a complex series of social events whose general characteristic is that they regulate matters of personal and institutional interest and value that are functionally important and strongly felt" (Hazard, 1965:47), lawyers are people who respond to an immense array of personal and institutional problems that vary from time to time, person to person, and place to place.

Thus, a lawyer's competence may be only peripherally connected with legal knowledge (Reuschemeyer, 1964). The image of "Mr. Fix It" is perhaps more descriptive of the role. Attorneys are called on to exercise a great deal of worldly knowledge in the process of solving client problems. They are frequently expected to act outside their specialty to provide business and economic advice, or provide clients with a sympathetic ear or organizational know-how.

Second, the roots of law practice lie deeply imbedded in the social, political, and economic institutions of a given society and a given community. Richard Wells grasps this principle in saying,

> The legal profession is one of those institutions which is secondary to and therefore dependent upon the primary economic and social institutions of the society. Given this situation, the actions . . . of the profession consist in response and service to primary institutions. (Wells, 1964:186).

Wells goes on to argue that the legal profession can be viewed as responding constantly to various stimuli. Thus as the primary institutions of a society or community change over time, so also will the character and the content of the practice of law. This is in contrast to the practice of medicine, where the roots of practice remain imbedded in the diseases and maladies of a discrete biological system. New discoveries both about diseases and their cures are constantly forthcoming, but the basic context of practice (the biological entity) remains unchanged. Law practice, on the other hand, not only reflects changing social conceptions of justice but alterations in economic institutions and political structures. The history of tort practice, for example, reflects a long journey within a relatively short time. While it is true that the idea of "civil wrongs" goes back to the Code of Hammurabi and the Talmud, and the common law roots of torts go back to the Middle Ages, it was the Industrial Revolution and especially the invention of the railroad locomotive that "breathed life into this ancient body" (Friedman, 1985:53). Changing social institutions have spread tort doctrine far beyond railroad accidents so that in 1978 a 24-year-old Boulder, Colorado, man felt entitled to sue his parents for $350,000, alleging that—in neglecting his needs for food, shelter, clothing, and psychological support—they were guilty of "malpractice of parenting" (64 *American Bar Association Journal,* 1978:961).

The roots of law practice are thrust particularly deep into the economic institutions of our society in general and into various community economic structures in particular. James C. Coleman (1982) calls our attention to the fact that the invention of the corporation as an actor in the social system has not only had a revolutionary impact on the economy, but produced an asymmetry of power in social relations. The "natural person" is a poor match for the immense power of the "corporate person." Thus in recent years, natural persons have sought to redress the balance of power by a variety of legal regulations on corporations—including truth in lending laws, privacy acts, and truth in advertising. A legal profession working in a society of small personal businesses will differ from a legal profession functioning in a society where economic actors are often larger in gross revenues than entire nations and where such entities are publicly owned.

Marc Galanter (1983) has further illustrated the extent to which developments in the institutional sector shape the contours of legal practice. He documents the emergence of "mega-lawyering" in response to the emergence of massive international corporations. Mega-lawyering involves larger firms with offices in several cities including foreign countries. It involves greater specialization of legal talent, more deliberate coordination of effort, and a team approach to client problems. "The growth of mega-lawyering is fostered by the proliferation of law and the consequent multiplication of the possibilities of legal manoeuvre" (Galanter, 1983:173). The proliferation of law is a response to the innovation and increase in complexity of economic institutions.

Our premise is that law practice is best understood as an externally determined social system. This is not to imply that other professions are unaffected by multiple influences from the social environments in which they practice. But it is to argue that there is a significant difference between, for example, the practice of medicine, which has its roots in the specific and bounded territory of biology—which is amenable to scientific inquiry for the sake of discovering causal relationships—and the practice of law, which has its roots deeply thrust into the shifting territory of social institutions where scientific methods may be used to chart the path of change, but where there is less confidence in the possibility of outlining a set of laws that govern institutional life. As Willard Hurst has so clearly pointed out,

> The most creative, driving and powerful pressures upon our law emerged from the social setting. Social environment has two aspects. First, it is what men think: how they size up the universe and their place in it; what things they value, and how much; what they believe to be the relations between cause and effect, and the way these ideas affect their notions of how to go about getting the things they value. What men do; their habits, their institutions. (Hurst, 1950:11)

Thus the practice of law throughout our history has closely reflected not only the main concerns of the society at any given time, but also the existing social and economic structures that typified a given period and/or setting. The struggle against malaria or cancer or heart disease or AIDS goes on with relative indifference to national boundaries, economic systems, or community size. But law practice has a much clearer contextual component. Securities specialists are unlikely to be found in Macon, Missouri. Divorce and personal injury practice may be found in Chicago as well as Centerville, but the meaning and mode of such a practice is quite different between the LaSalle Street practitioners and their Main Street colleagues.

THE ECOLOGY OF LAW PRACTICE

If one argues that the legal profession represents an externally determined social system, then a corollary suggests that there is an ecology of law practice. Ecology, in its most general sense, deals with the relationship between organisms and their environment. Human ecology proceeds on the assumption that the differential spatial distribution of human actors produces differential adaptations to the environment and these adaptations are a collective rather than an individual process (Hawley, 1986:186).

An ecological frame of reference suggests, for example, that city size can be used as a sociological variable (Ogburn and Duncan, 1964). It suggests that community structure can be analyzed ecologically (Hawley, 1950). Organizations reflect differences based on variations in population ecology (Carroll, 1984; Hannan and Freeman, 1977). Complexity of social organization can be tied to population size (Carniero, 1967). These illustrate only a few of the applications of ecological theory.

Within the rural-urban frame of reference, an ecological approach to social phenomena is based on the following logic:

1. Rural areas are considered to be smaller in population, lower in density, less complex, and more homogeneous than urban areas.
2. These ecological differences are consequential for the sociocultural life of rural and urban residents.

3. The differences in size, density, complexity, and heterogeneity act in a linear fashion as one shifts from the smallest, simplest rural areas to the largest, most complex, urban agglomeration (Van Es and Brown, 1974).

Such a set of propositions leads us to suspect that there are significant differences within the legal profession between urban and nonurban practitioners. Those differences, given the fact that legal practice is deeply rooted in the highly variable institutions of a containing community, are likely to be seen not only in what lawyers do but how they go about doing it. A hint of this is seen in the fact that one in seven lawyers in New York City do not appear in court at all and 40 percent spend less than two hours a week there, while rural lawyers speak of nearly daily trips to the courthouse. As one lawyer expressed it, "Here in the country, litigation is the name of the game."

THE VARIABLES ASSOCIATED WITH THE ECOLOGY OF LAW PRACTICE

If we proceed on the assumption that the bar is an externally determined social system and that there may therefore be an ecology of law practice that further fragments the legal profession, what variables can we reasonably deduce will be associated with such variations in content as well as manner of law practice? More directly, what specific characteristics of the small-town, rural setting are likely to produce what kinds of differences in the structure and practice patterns of the nonurban bar? How does context shape professional conduct?

Two primary variables will be examined: (1) economic scale, and (2) population scale. Whatever disagreements exist among social scientists about the lack of distinction between rural and urban contexts, there is agreement that population size and economic scale are clearly different in the two settings.

ECONOMIC SCALE AND THE PRACTICE OF LAW

Cities represent vast concentrations of wealth. One factor contributing to this is the symbiotic relationship that has developed between cities and corporations in the twentieth century. The result is not only an economics of immense scale but also a metropolitanization of decision making. Increasingly, the decisions and actions of greatest consequence to the society are controlled and made by corporate actors. This includes not only private corporations but also the public bureaucracies that regulate and serve them. The vast majority of these actors are in metropolitan places.

Coleman (1982) has documented the emergence of these new actors in society and the resulting asymmetry of power between natural persons and the new corporate persons. Legal activity and business activity have always been intimately linked together (Zemans and Rosenblum, 1981:65). But what is different is the eclipse of natural persons as actors in the business scene by corporate persons. In 1853, for example, only 15 percent of the actors in court cases were corporations. The vast majority (85 percent) were individuals. But by 1973 the ratio had changed dramatically. In that year 58 percent of court cases involved corporate actors (Coleman, 1982:11, 12).

The most visible impact of corporate-scale economic activity is the emergence of the large, departmentalized law firm found in metropolitan settings (Heinz and Laumann, 1982:18, 19). Teams of attorneys with highly specialized expertise are assembled to serve the vast array of legal issues faced by their corporate clients. The traditional general-practice lawyer has no place in this enterprise.

But the impact of cities on law practice is not limited to the uniqueness of corporate representation. Natural persons in cities also tend to be different. On the average their incomes are higher, they are better educated, they are more likely to be in professional-managerial occupations, and they are more likely to own property—all of which tend to generate law business of a particular character. A community's economic base influences the manner and style in which its residents live (Bollens and Schmandt, 1982:64). Higher income people are more likely to seek legal representation for property acquisitions, tax representation, and estate services (Mayhew and Reiss, 1969). Lower income persons are more frequently involved in "personal plight" issues of criminal defense, divorce, and personal injury (Carlin, 1962).

The city, because of its immense economic scale, is the locus of mega-lawyering. It is the context of large legal organizations, "manned by specialist functionaries guided by recondite learning, accessible only through imposing intermediaries. . . . The majesty of mega-law is imparted not by wigs, robes and gibbets, but by files, experts and computers massed in assemblages beyond the span of personal experience and beyond the grasp of personal understanding" (Galanter, 1983:166).

There is nothing to approximate mega-lawyering in small towns. The economic base is not there. The corporate actors are not likely to have their headquarters there. Smaller towns remain the province of natural persons. It is not that the actions of corporate persons do not impact small towns. They do. But the central actors in the corporate drama are elsewhere.

Given the more modest economic scale of the rural, small-town environment, it seems logical to assume that law practice there would contrast with urban practice in several respects. Such contrast would include the following dimensions:

1. *Client mix.* While metropolitan practice is "corporate-intensive" practice, small town practice will likely be "person-intensive" practice. The bulk of small town clients will probably be individuals, and small town lawyers would derive the greatest proportion of their income from representing persons.
2. *Cases and issues.* If small town practice is person-intensive practice, then the bulk of legal effort will tend to be devoted to issues important to individuals. This will include such matters as family law and divorce, criminal defense, personal injury,

and real estate. One would expect the small town attorney's typical practice to consist of a large volume of small matters while the typical metropolitan lawyer will have a small volume of relatively large matters.

3. *Practice style*. Whereas the scale and complexity of economic activity in metropolitan settings tends to produce specialized law practice focused in large law firms, the norm in small settings will likely be general practice carried out in an entrepreneurial (solo or small firm) mode. While the growing complexities of law practice may press country lawyers to restrict their practice, the economic realities would make it only rarely feasible to specialize.
4. *Structure of the bar*. The scale and complexity of the metropolitan setting produces a fragmented and highly stratified bar. The hierarchy is dictated by clientele differences and is reflected in differentials in lawyer income, status, and power. Because the range of client differences is greatly reduced in smaller towns, we would expect a relatively less stratified bar. The opportunity to serve an exclusive clientele in the country is reduced by the reduced scale of the economy and the population. Thus, we would anticipate that rural attorneys will have remarkably similar clienteles with quite similar problems. The "moral division of labor" seen in metropolitan settings is not likely to be experienced in smaller settings.
5. *Accountability*. If the core clients of country practitioners come from individuals in the community rather than from corporate or business entities, it appears that country lawyers would experience a higher level of accountability in their practice. The necessity to serve a large number of small clients means enhanced exposure to criticism. Such criticism coupled with small-town communication systems would appear to constitute a significant threat to practitioners' reputations and thus to their business.
6. *Lawyer autonomy*. Research in metropolitan settings suggests that lawyers serving elite corporate clientele tend to have less professional autonomy (Heinz and Laumann, 1982:359–60). Because of the immense volume of business from a single client, the firm sacrifices some of its independence to retain the lucrative business. We would presume that, in smaller settings where lawyers depend on a high volume of business from a variety of relatively infrequent players in the system, attorneys would retain considerable autonomy over their practice and escape the dilemma of large client dependence.

POPULATION SCALE AND THE PRACTICE OF LAW

By definition, small towns are different from metropolitan settings along a second dimension: population size. In some respects economic scale and population size are deeply intertwined. But there are some consequences for law practice that are linked directly to population size; they can be outlined here and elaborated later when the data are examined.

Size of the Practicing Bar

In large cities the number of lawyers is immense. In 1981 the ratio of lawyers to the population of the country as a whole was 1:403 (Curran, 1985:366). By contrast, in rural North Dakota the ratio of lawyers to population was 1:888, less than half the national average and only one-tenth the ratio found in Boston (Curran, 1985:442). If the ratio of lawyers to population in smaller towns is relatively small, there are corollary effects we are likely to find.

1. Because there are relatively few lawyers per community, the probability of conflict-of-interest problems increases. A lawyer who has regularly served a local hardware dealer is not likely to accept as a client a person who has a complaint against the dealer. Under such conditions local businesses might be able to co-opt the best lawyers in town and effectively ward off the likelihood of litigation.
2. Whereas the bar in large cities is highly stratified and fragmented as well as too large to permit frequent interaction and close collegial ties, the rural bar is likely to be small enough to cultivate a sense of community. Rural practitioners would be likely to interact on a daily basis. Also, because of the necessity to refer matters to colleagues in avoiding potential conflicts of interest, an interdependence is likely to emerge—creating a substantial professional solidarity in the country setting that is not seen in metropolitan settings. This ever-present possibility of conflict of interest might also tend to discourage firm practice since, in smaller settings with few attorneys, the probability of two attorneys in the same firm being asked to represent opposing parties to an issue is substantially higher than in larger settings.

The Meaning of Practice Patterns

The hierarchical organization of the bar in metropolitan settings produces a "moral division of labor" that is discrediting to practitioners who serve individuals instead of corporate or business clients (Carlin, 1962; Hughes, 1958:71). Because there are elite corporate clients in sufficient numbers in large cities to allow some practitioners to restrict their practice exclusively to them, other practitioners who represent less remunerative and more routine individual client matters are relegated to an inferior status within the profession. In the country, such a division of labor does not appear feasible. Consequently, client loads would tend to be similar among all attorneys. Because individual clients and their more routine problems are the norm, such work is not likely to be seen as discrediting.

The Expanded Lawyer Role

The metropolitan center with its vast population base represents an opportunity for establishing a variety of professional personal services running all the way from psychologists, management consultants, and investment advisors to social workers, professionally trained clergy, and occupational therapists. Small towns can rarely support such an array of human services. Thus it is likely that the role of the lawyer in such a setting will expand significantly beyond legal counseling. Citizens may tend to expect the local attorney to fill many roles because of the dearth of professional practitioners available in smaller settings.

Socioeconomic Characteristics of Rural Clients

We have already alluded to the fact that there is a significant relationship between rural settings and the socioeconomic status of the population. Not only are rural citizens in possession of less income and less education than urban dwellers, they also tend to be older. Thus we would expect attorneys in small towns to handle a high proportion of legal problems typical of less educated, older, and more economically marginal citizens. This would include entitlement issues, estate matters, domestic and divorce matters, criminal defense, and other personal plight issues.

The Predominance of Multiplex Relationships

Human relationships vary by the size of the context in which they occur. In dense urban settings "single interest" relationships are common. You know John Jones, your dentist, only in the context of dentistry. You are unlikely to belong to the same club he does or live in the same neighborhood. Your encounters with him typically occur in the dentist's chair and nowhere else.

Such is not true, however, in smaller settings. Here relationships tend to be more "multiplex" (Gluckman, 1955:19). Because population density is lower and people encounter each other more frequently, it is more likely you will encounter and interact with others in a variety of roles. In the small setting John Jones may not only be your dentist, but you may also serve with him on the local church board. His children are likely to attend the same school your children attend, and because there is only one service club in town you two are likely to meet at Kiwanis on Thursdays.

This multiplex quality of relationships in small settings means that you are likely to share a variety of interests with others. Relationships would tend to transcend the formal roles of attorney and client. While you come to the local attorney because of his professional skill, it is likely you come to him as a friend as well. Your interaction at any instant impinges on a variety of interests in addition to the one currently being addressed.

It is likely, therefore, that in rural settings attorney-client relationships will be multiplex. That fact will likely produce higher levels of professional accountability because more than a single interest is at stake in any transaction. Multiplicity also involves significant overlap in friendships, which increases the vulnerability of country lawyers. If they serve a client poorly, the word gets around quickly.

On the other hand, rural lawyers, who are so likely to see their clients in a variety of roles, are in a position to serve clients' interests in a context of greater knowledge. They are likely to know each client's family, associates, and perhaps even health and finances.

Multiplex relationships in small towns may also tend to create an expectation of lawyer accessibility that would not be typical of larger settings. If, in addition to being one's lawyer, the attorney is also a friend or an associate, then the lawyer's office is not exclusively a place for technical discussions and legal appointments. It may be expected to have an open door much of the time.

Multiplex relationships may also tend to increase the likelihood of conflicts of interest for country lawyers. If you are asked by a business client to collect a debt from a fellow Rotarian, you may be likely to refer the client to another attorney in order to preserve the Rotarian's friendship.

In short, multiplex relationships tend to make discrete roles more diffuse. In a metropolitan setting the lawyer is more likely to be seen as a technical expert. In the smaller setting there may be strong forces transforming the lawyer's identity to that of friend.

The Less Regulated Setting

Densely populated areas require greater regulation of individual behavior. Local ordinances regulating traffic, zoning, building, noise, parking, rent, business licenses, and so forth tend to proliferate as the problems of scale develop. In smaller settings there are fewer regulations required. Consequently, individual clients in smaller settings are likely to bring more personal-plight issues to attorneys than they will local rule-related cases, which might be more typical of urban settings.

The Intimacy of the Small Setting

Joseph Lyford, commenting about life in a small town, recalls this conversation:

> "Nobody could ever die in Vandalia and not be missed right away," says one complainer, "but sometimes I think I'd prefer a big city. At least you can live without being noticed, even if you may decay in your apartment for several days after you're dead." (Lyford, 1965:10, 11)

Such is the image, if not the reality, of intimacy in small towns. It is not that intimacy does not occur in cities. It does (Fischer, 1982). But it is perceived as pervasive in small settings. Lingeman (1980:287) recalls the local resistance to adding street numbers to houses in small towns—because it implied that everyone did not know everyone else. The anecdotes about face-to-face relationships in small towns are numberless.

Intimacy is apparently more than image in small towns. S. S. Gutterman (1969) found intimacy negatively correlated with size of community. Social interactions based on face-to-face contact that also extend backward over time are clearly more personalized and immediate and less categoric than the status-to-status interactions that typify the general pattern in larger urban centers.

Small town intimacy has been observed to strip the political process of its ideological component (Ladd, 1969:87). Politics in small towns tend to be personalized. James Williams described politics in Waterbury, New York, in the early years of the twentieth century by saying, "Town officials were chosen not for their ability to administer the affairs of their office efficiently as much as for their personal impressiveness" (1906:60). Arthur Vidich and Joseph Bensman (1968:130) found local politicians in Springdale, New York (pseudonym), avoiding issues or positions that might alienate them from other notables with whom they must get along month after month on a friendly basis.

How might the perceived intimacy of relationships in a small town affect law practice there?

1. Face-to-face interactions generate, maintain, and alter reputations in intimate settings. The country lawyer is likely to be deeply appreciative of the role of reputation in his law business. Community standards and expectations, if not already internalized, are likely to be understood and respected. Lawyers are not likely to offend community standards. Nor are they likely to bring a malpractice suit against a local physician or a dress-code violation suit against the local school board. The image, if not the reality, in small towns is one of community: shared values, understood rules, and substantial solidarity. Those principles are indeed violated in small settings, but not routinely or without conscious reflection on the possible consequences. Because the country lawyer's success lies in maintaining a good reputation with the whole community, it is likely that community standards and expectations will be influential in the kinds of cases and matters handled and in the way they are handled. While rural practitioners may enjoy a greater professional autonomy because they are not so likely to be dependent on a few large clients as their big-city colleagues may be, they have their own problems of independence because of their intimate ties to a face-to-face community.
2. Because small settings make it possible for persons to interact with each other more frequently, there is an intrinsic pressure toward defining acquaintances as "friends" (Homans, 1950:133). Thus country lawyers are likely to have a more diffuse identity than their metropolitan counterparts. Client-lawyer interaction in the country is likely to proceed on a basis that defines the practitioner both as legal expert and personal friend. Rural attorneys are likely to be judged on the quality of their performance in both roles.
3. Overall, the country practitioner works in a setting in which intimacy, accessibility, and accountability are inextricably bound together.

Community Participation in the Smaller Setting

There appear to be a number of factors that would draw country lawyers into extensive involvement in civic and community activities, in contrast to the level of involvement of their metropolitan peers.

First, the opportunity for deep involvement in the activities and affairs of the organized profession are reduced in small settings. Typically, the bar has only rudimentary organization at the local level because of small numbers. Even at the circuit level, activities are infrequent and predominantly social. On the other hand, the bar is highly organized in metropolitan settings (Heinz and Laumann, 1982:211–309) and provides opportunity for a broad range of professional activities that carry considerable rewards and recognition to participants. Being less structured, the rural bar is less able to reward participants. This fact may lead members of the small town bar to invest themselves emotionally, socially, and economically in the local community—because it is a more viable source of reward and recognition.

Second, there may be considerable pressure from local citizens for attorneys to take leadership roles in local affairs. The country lawyer may be the best-educated person in town. Because lawyers are professionals and because the setting is more provincial, they may still be looked on as "possessing a broad culture, a wide special competence, and a general understanding of affairs" whereas, in the metropolitan setting, the meaning of being professional has been transformed so that they "are regarded by the public as experts—persons with high competence in a restricted sphere. Outside their role, they are thought to have no more claim to be heard than the man on the street" (Carr-Sanders, 1955:286–87). This metropolitanization of professionals is less likely to have extended to settings where professional numbers are smaller, and where there may be greater deference shown to them. Because of the local perception of lawyers in small towns, we would anticipate that a considerable measure of local leadership would be available to them if they wished to take it.

There is a strong likelihood that rural lawyers would respond to the opportunity to be involved in the leadership of their communities. It is a source of recognition and reward not available in professional associations. But perhaps more importantly, the welfare of the practitioner and the welfare of the community are closely tied together. Getting involved in the community means protecting one's own interests. Promoting the economic welfare of a small community means generating more potential clients. The probability of this kind of linkage with the community is greater in small settings, where systems are less complex and community vulnerability is better understood (Bellah et al., 1985:167–95). In particular, attorneys who have been raised in the community are likely to define their identity in terms of it, which means that the interests of the community and of the attorney would be parallel.

Finally, there is also the likelihood that community activity and visibility may enhance the growth of a practice. Running for political office, displaying one's trial skills as prosecuting attorney, or leading the local Democrats may be effective ways of inaugurating a practice in a small setting.

Overall, we would expect to find the level of community activity higher among country practitioners. We would also expect to find their assessment of the personal importance of community leadership to be higher than their metropolitan colleagues.

Localized Legal Culture

Legal pluralism—the appearance of variations within the legal system even where a common set of rules provides for consistency—has been widely documented. David Engel (1984) describes how people in Sander Country, Illinois (pseudonym) see contract default as a much more compelling reason for legal redress than personal injury issues. He also documents the local legal culture of divorce proceedings within the same community (Engel, 1980). Carol Greenhouse (1982) describes the avoidance of litigation within a conservative religious community, despite the growing propensity of the larger society to sue. Richard Wells (1970) has documented the impact of local values and practices on the legal process. Frances Zemans (1982:1018) shows how group norms impact the decision to use law as a remedy.

Not only is there a plurality of practices within single legal systems, but it appears that the smaller settings show legal processing to be quite particularistic while larger settings tend to reflect more universalistic practices (Engel, 1984). As the scale of a social system enlarges, it tends to rely more on formal rules to produce the integration of its varied parts. It is not surprising therefore to hear metropolitan lawyers "going by the book" in interactions with their counterparts in the larger settings. Because their interactions with any specific lawyer may be less frequent and because there is such a vast array of potential counterparts, a clear set of rules must be set forth for all. In smaller settings, informal rule systems are more likely to occur. The smaller the size of the bar, the more frequent are the members' interactions with each other. This would be likely to produce a set of informal rules understood by all the locals, but perhaps at variance with practice elsewhere. Therefore, we would expect country lawyers to develop informal understandings about how their work with each other is to proceed. Such understandings are likely to be instruments of efficiency, given the anticipated character of rural practice—a high volume of smaller matters. It would be important to country lawyers not to be overburdened with paperwork, interrogatories, and discovery on matters that will yield only modest fees. Thus we would expect to find local understandings that would contrast significantly with the rule systems followed in settings where the lawyer population is more dense and the structure of the bar more complex.

SUMMARY

We have argued that the legal profession is an externally determined social system. It derives its structure not only from the common socialization the profession receives in law school, but more importantly from the context in which practice occurs. As a profession, the bar is thus likely to reflect the variations of context more visibly than many other forms of professional practice. Part of the reason for this extreme sensitivity to context lies in the fact that the practice of law is not a science rooted in principles and structures that are essentially invariant in nature, as—for example—is the practice of medicine. Rather, the practice of law is rooted in the varied and changing character of human institutions. Its roots are imbedded in the character of a local economy. Its issues represent the social and political preferences of a discrete population. Its procedures are invented and altered under the dictates of immediate situations. Thus even within a single large metropolitan area there are multiple professions of law, depending on which segment of the population is being addressed.

We have suggested, therefore, that there may be an ecology of law practice. The practice of law in small rural settings is apt to be significantly different from the practice of law in large urban contexts. The primary variables differentiating the rural from the metropolitan context are population scale and economic scale. The differences in scale suggest that country practice will mirror conditions in significant contrast to those in which metropolitan practice are rooted.

Specifically, we suggested that, because of the differences in economic scale, one might anticipate a unique client mix in rural areas that is person-intensive in contrast to the more entity-intensive character of metropolitan practice. We anticipated that the preponderance of cases in rural practice would fall into the personal plight category. Practice style is more likely to be entrepreneurial than institutional, and—as a consequence—the bar is less likely to be rigidly and steeply stratified. We also anticipated that, while a preponderance of individual clients within a small intimate setting would likely lead to relatively higher levels of accountability on the part of rural practitioners, there is also a likelihood that country lawyers—who are less likely to be tied to a single, highly remunerative client—may also experience greater autonomy in their practice than is typical of institutional practitioners.

We hypothesized that the reduced population scale in rural settings would not only produce a small, collegial, interdependent bar, but also expand the likelihood of conflict-of-interest problems. The more homogeneous population in small towns would mean that lawyers' clients tend to be similar, which reduces the likelihood of a moral division of labor developing there as it has in the urban bar. The smaller population tends to increase the likelihood of multiplex relationships in a small town. Such relationships might make the attorney's role more diffuse. Coupled with the relative absence of other personal service professionals in small towns, the role of the lawyer as general counselor and friend is apt to become expanded over what may generally be found in urban settings. The fact that human relationships in more intimate settings tend to be person-to-person rather than status-to-status also places greater emphasis on the accessibility and accountability of the practitioner. Finally, we suggested that in the smaller setting the lawyer is likely to be more deeply involved in civic affairs, giving leadership and receiving the coveted prize of recognition in return.

From this framework of understanding, we propose that there is indeed an ecology of law practice. To more thoroughly test that general proposition as well as the specific hypotheses outlined above, we turn now to the data.

2

A PROFILE OF THE RURAL BAR

The country lawyer practicing in the smallest settings in Missouri is typically a male in his early 40s who was born and raised in the county where he is currently practicing. He is Caucasian, Protestant, and thinks of himself as a Democrat. His father is as likely to have been a blue-collar worker or farmer as he is to have been a lawyer, administrator-manager, or other professional. The country lawyer was educated in the state and graduated from the law school at the University of Missouri in Columbia. He has practiced solo at some time in his career, and currently is either a solo practitioner or in a two-to-three person firm. His office is located downtown on or near Main Street with easy access to the county courthouse or title company. He will do work for 350 or more clients a year, which he considers too many. He will work 48 hours a week or more and earn between $50,000 and $60,000 (1981 dollars) a year from his law practice.

His clients will be largely individuals rather than organizations or businesses and are as likely to be blue-collar workers as they are to hold managerial or professional jobs. The majority of his income will derive from practice in three areas: estate, domestic relations, and negligence (plaintiff); but he describes himself as a general practitioner. Besides his law practice he will be involved in one or more additional entrepreneurial activities ranging from farming, real estate development, and construction to cable TV, newspaper publishing, and traveling carnival management.

It is unlikely that he will belong to the ABA, and he is relatively uninterested in professional activities at the national level. However, he does see leadership roles in the Missouri Bar as important to him, as is local community leadership.

He is involved in a half-dozen or more local organizations including social, civic, and religious groups. He typically attends church two to three times a month and has been elected to political office at least once. He sees election or appointment to the judiciary as a desirable climax to his career.

Such a profile does erase the variation within the rural bar, and variation is both present and important. However, the general picture that emerges is a bar that is fundamentally homogeneous. The homogeneity embraces practitioners' backgrounds as well as their current practice situations, client loads, and work situations.

THE IMPACT OF CONTEXT

Virtually all of the studies of the bar in metropolitan contexts have noted the heterogeneity of the profession (Carlin, 1962, 1966; Ladinsky, 1963; Heinz and Laumann, 1982). Beginning with diverse ethno-religious backgrounds, metropolitan practitioners reflect significantly diverse law school experiences—culminating in extreme contrasts in practice settings and clientele. Metropolitan populations themselves are more ethnically and religiously diverse, and to the extent that law practice is a source of upward mobility it is no surprise that the practicing bar should reflect the ethno-religious mix of the containing community. Nor is it surprising that the more homogeneous rural communities should produce a similarly homogeneous bar.

But our orienting question is, how many facets of the legal profession and its work reflect the contextual impact? Is there indeed an ecology of law practice? We will examine this question by comparing data from three different settings. The data from the Chicago study represent the metropolitan context. The data from rural Missouri represent the opposite extreme: the small town setting. In between these two extremes are the data from Springfield, Missouri—a middle-size city (155,000). The three data sets enable us to determine if there is indeed something approximating a linear relationship between law practice characteristics in small settings and those in metropolitan settings. Do changes begin to appear as one moves from the smallest settings to the middle-size setting, and then become more dramatic as one moves to the metropolitan setting? The data will be arrayed to enable such an analysis.

To further enhance the analysis, the Chicago data will be broken down to show a segment of the bar—the "corporate cluster"—that is least like the rural bar, as well as the other extreme—the "personal plight cluster"—that is nearest to the rural bar, at least in clientele characteristics. Such a breakdown of the metropolitan data should help us to see how similar at least a segment of the metropolitan bar is to the rural bar.

SOCIAL BACKGROUND

The data in Table 2.1 suggest that the metropolitan bar is somewhat older than the rural bar and much more likely to have female and non-white practi-

Table 2.1
Social Background of Lawyers

Practice Settings	Number of Respondents (1)	% Male (2)	% Female (3)	Mean Age (4)	% Metropolitan Origin (5)	% Rural Origin (6)	% Caucasian (7)	% Non-religious (8)	% Protestant (9)	% Catholic (10)	% Jewish (11)	% Republican (12)	% Democrat (13)	% Independent (14)	% Fathers Administrators or Professionals (15)	% Fathers Lawyers (16)
Rural Missouri	201	99	1	43	6	87	100	2	83	14	0	38	55	7	39	16
Springfield, Missouri	77	96	4	42	7	58	100	17	77	6	0	46	31	23	45	16
Chicago (total sample)	777	96	4	44	78	ND	98	12	25	30	33	22	37	41	72	15
Large Corporate Cluster	151	ND	ND	41	72	ND	99	16	26	29	28	22	34	44	71	12
Personal Plight Cluster	171	ND	ND	44	93	ND	94	14	12	33	42	7	64	29	65	14

Source: Chicago data are from Heinz and Laumann, 1982. Reprinted with permission.

tioners. That is not a remarkable finding. Not only are blacks less likely to be found in small towns in Missouri, but also the conservative sentiment of rural areas is not likely to draw female pioneers to open law practices in strongly traditional settings. In fact, the proportion of female practitioners in both Springfield and Chicago suggests that the relationship between context and gender of practitioners is in the expected direction.

The data also suggest that both the Chicago and the rural bars are essentially native grown. More than three-fourths of the Chicago bar were raised in a metropolitan setting while 87 percent of the rural bar were raised in the country or in small towns. As one might expect, the lower status "personal plight sector" of the metropolitan bar is more locally grown than the "large corporate sector," which because of its elite status tends to draw practitioners from a wider geographical area.

The religious background of the contrasting bars is also a microcosm of the larger setting. Eastern European Jewish practitioners represent one-third of the Chicago bar—reflecting their substantial presence in the city as a whole. No Jewish practitioners are found in rural Missouri or Springfield. The smaller settings are decidedly Protestant while the metropolitan setting is about evenly divided between Protestant and Catholic—again typical of the rural-urban continuum.

Somewhat surprising is the finding that, in the conservative rural area, lawyers are decidedly more Democratic in political orientation than Republican. However, attitudinal data—to be discussed later—clearly reflect the traditional rural conservatism, despite the political identification.

The vast majority (87 percent) of the Chicago lawyers' fathers were either administrators, managers, professionals, or lawyers. The rural bar shows only 55 percent with such a background. The Springfield bar stands midway between the two extremes. Because the proportion of managerial-professional jobs available in rural areas is considerably less than the proportion in more urban areas, the difference is not so surprising. But it does indicate that a higher proportion of the rural bar are using law practice as a means of upward mobility.

The metropolitan bar has a much more cosmopolitan educational background than the rural bar. Table 2.2 data show that there is a compelling homogeneity of background in the rural bar. Seventy percent graduated from the University of Missouri Law School in Columbia. Another 10 percent graduated from the University of Missouri Law School in Kansas City. Still another 10 percent attended either Washington University or St. Louis University law schools in St. Louis. The Chicago bar, with its extensive corporate practice, has 20 percent of its practitioners from elite law schools. The kind of homogeneity reflected in the law school backgrounds of the rural bar is most nearly approximated by the personal plight cluster of the Chicago bar. Sixty-four percent of them are graduates of local Chicago law schools.

The general conclusion we can draw from the social background data is that there is an essential symmetry between the characteristics of the bar and the

Table 2.2
Law School Background, by Practice Setting (percent)

Practice Settings	N (1)	Elite Schools (2)	Prestige Schools (3)	Regional Schools (4)	Local Schools (5)
Rural Missouri	201	1	0	92	7
Springfield, MO	77	1	0	87	12
Chicago (Total)	699	20	17	16	45
Corporate	151	28	18	22	32
Personal Plight	171	12	9	13	64

Source: Chicago data are from Heinz and Laumann, 1982. Reprinted with permission.
(2) Elite schools include University of Chicago, Columbia, Harvard, Michigan, Stanford and Yale.
(3) Prestige schools include University of California (Berkeley), Cornell, Georgetown, New York University, Northwestern, University of Pennsylvania, University of Virginia, and University of Wisconsin.
(4) Regional schools include all schools not included in the elite, prestige or local groupings. For the Chicago data, the most numerous in this category are graduates from the University of Illinois. In the rural Missouri data and Springfield data, the vast majority are graduates of the University of Missouri law schools at Columbia and Kansas City.
(5) Local schools in the Chicago sample include DePaul University, Chicago Kent, Loyola University and John Marshall. In the rural and Springfield sample, the category refers to proprietary law schools and schools of lesser status than state university schools (e.g. Memphis State, Washburn, Oklahoma City University, St. Mary's University, Gonzaga, University of Tulsa, etc.).

demographic characteristics of the containing community. This is true largely because each of the bars is decidedly ''local''—drawn from the context in which they currently practice. They reflect the socioeconomic profiles of their larger communities as well as the primary ethno-religious characteristics of the context. In short, the bar does appear to mirror its containing community.

PRACTICE TYPE

The data in Table 2.3 dramatically show the impact of context on practice type. In larger settings where the variety of clients as well as the absolute number of clients is relatively large, and where corporate clients needing a variety of legal services are numerous, it is not surprising to see almost 20 percent of the lawyers practicing in firms of more than 30 lawyers. Such large firms symbolize specialized law practice in an institutional setting. At the other extreme where specialization is hardly feasible, 88 percent of the rural attorneys practice alone or in two-to-three person firms. That proportion drops to 44 percent in Springfield where specialization and corporate practice is more feasible. Again there is an essential symmetry between setting and practice type. Where large organizations dominate the landscape, large law firms mirroring their clients' scale emerge to serve their needs. In settings where individuals and small businesses predominate, individual practitioners and small partnerships are the rule. While such a sym-

Table 2.3
Firm Size Characteristics, by Practice Setting

Practice Settings	Number of Practitioner Respondents (1)	% Solo Practitioners (2)	% 2-3 Person Firms (3)	% 4-5 Person Firms (4)	% 6-9 Person Firms (5)	% 2-9 Person Firms (6)	% 10-30 Person Firms (7)	% 30 or More Person Firms (8)	% with Additional Vocations (9)	Median Hours Worked Per Week (10)	Average Years In Practice (11)
Rural Missouri	201	43	45	10	1	56	1	0	55	48	15.1
Springfield, MO.	77	34	13	14	12	39	27	0	25	43	14.4
Chicago (total)	699	21	*	*	*	26	10	17	*	*	*
Large Corporate Cluster	150	6	*	*	*	11	12	44	*	*	*
Personal Plight Cluster	138	42	*	*	*	36	3	3	*	*	*

Source: Chicago data are from Heinz and Laumann, 1982. Reprinted with permission.
*No data

biotic relationship is not surprising, it does again suggest the dependent relationship of law practice on the characteristics of the containing community.

The preponderance of entrepreneurial (solo) practice in the rural setting may help to explain the high frequency (55 percent) with which rural practitioners engage in additional entrepreneurial activities. Most lawyers both in rural Missouri and in Springfield indicate that they have outside investments. But the rural bar is unique in the degree to which additional business undertakings requiring their time and management skills are built in addition to their law practices. The interviews gave the distinct impression that rural attorneys are fundamentally entrepreneurs; law practice is but one, if not the primary, expression of their entrepreneurial orientation. One attorney in a town of 12,000 who was heavily involved in construction and real estate development said, "My law practice is my source of capital for my construction and real estate development ventures. It's a nice combination."

Entrepreneurial practice is as much an adaptation to the circumstances of rural practice as institutional (large firm) practice is an adaptation to the circumstances of large-scale settings. Again, the contours of the profession appear to mirror the contours of the community.

CLIENT CHARACTERISTICS

Client characteristics are but the obverse side of practice type for attorneys. In the large metropolitan setting where large business and corporate clients create institutional practice, we would expect the number of such clients per practitioner

Table 2.4
Client Characteristics, by Practice Setting

Practice Settings	(Number of Respondents) (1)	(Median # of Clients per year) (2)	(Median % of personal clients) (3)	(Mean # of clients bringing personal matters) (4)	(Mean % of Blue Collar Clients) (5)	(Mean % of Business Income From Major Corporate Clients (6)
Rural Missouri	201	350	86	314	45	8
Springfield, MO	77	150	62	147	39	24
Chicago (Total)	699	35	no data	no data	13	35
Corporate Cluster	151	25	no data	no data	2	62
Personal Plight Cluster	171	100	no data	no data	34	10

Source: Chicago data from Heinz and Laumann, 1982. Reprinted with permission.

to be relatively few, compared to rural settings. The data in Table 2.4 show the extent of the contrast. The median number of clients served per practitioner in rural areas is 350 whereas in Chicago it is precisely one-tenth that number. Springfield, as might be anticipated, stands about midway between the two extremes.

In the country, clients are predominantly persons. Such clientele bring a large number of small matters to attorneys—wills, real estate contracts, divorces, adoptions, consumer complaints, criminal defense work, and so forth. In fact, of the 350 clients coming annually to a rural lawyer, 314 (90 percent) of them—on the average—will be individuals.

In Springfield, by contrast, the median percent of individual clients drops to 62 percent of the total number of clients. The annual number of clients drops to less than half (150) of the rural median number (350). What we are observing here is the increasing salience of business and corporate clients in the larger setting where the ratio of large businesses and corporations to population is much higher. The available client mix in small settings is skewed to individuals—hence lawyers' client loads will reflect that. The larger the setting, the more skewed is the client mix to larger businesses and corporations—and consequently, that becomes the norm in urban practice. This raises the question of where the individual needing legal service is most likely to be adequately served. The answer is not so obvious as it may seem, since there are many factors that affect the quality and availability of service. But an individual visiting the rural attorney's office will certainly not appear as an exception among the other clients on the country lawyer's appointment book.

Clients in the country are also more likely to be blue-collar folk (45 percent) than in either Springfield (39 percent) or Chicago (13 percent). But again, the ratio is a reflection of the context. There are fewer white-collar jobs in rural settings, so a higher proportion of prospective clients will be wage workers. The data also suggest an increasing probability of business-client income coming from major corporate clients as one moves to the larger settings. This, again, is consistent with out expectations.

According to the data, client mix is a function of community size. The smaller the setting, the fewer entities there are for lawyers to represent—so their practice adapts to individual clients. Such clients become the rule—in contrast to the urban setting, where the entity-individual ratio is reversed. Even if the ratio were not reversed in the urban setting, the generally greater profitability of doing business and corporate law work would probably draw at least a large proportion of practitioners into such practice in preference to "people practice." The rural lawyers, then—with narrower options—make a law practice out of the available materials. In large settings where materials are more numerous and differentiated (individuals as well as organizations, businesses, government, and corporations), the most lucrative clients are picked up first and the less remunerative practice is left to a substratum of the bar (Carlin, 1962:22–23).

Of particular interest is the apparent relationship between the Chicago personal plight cluster and the rural sample. They both have high numbers of clients—a large proportion of whom are blue collar. They both receive very little of their business income from large corporate clients. Do similarities in clients create similarity in practice patterns? Or, again, does community context produce its unique effect and make the similarity more apparent than real? That intriguing question will be taken up in the next chapter.

PRACTICE CHARACTERISTICS

It would seem apparent that lawyers practicing in different areas of the law would use different kinds of professional expertise. The personal injury lawyer will be called on to negotiate with insurance companies and to try cases in court. The criminal defense lawyer negotiates with the prosecuting attorney and also tries cases. The lawyer specializing in corporate mergers or tax matters may rarely appear in court. He or she will need to use highly technical skills. To get a sense for how context may affect the kind of professional skills used by lawyers, we asked the rural and the Springfield bars to respond to seven pairs of statements to which the Chicago bar had earlier responded. The results are displayed in Table 2.5.

The first pair of statements, reported in column (2), has to do with whether the attorney's practice is more involved with highly technical procedures as opposed to a practice where negotiating and advising clients is the norm. Not surprisingly, a majority of the rural practitioners saw their practices as involving the interpersonal skills of negotiation and advising, as opposed to a detailed

Table 2.5
Practice Characteristics, by Practice Setting

Practice Setting	Number of Respondents (1)	% High Negotiating and Advising (2)	% High on Technical Expertise (3)	% High Specialization of Work (4)	% High Change in Law (5)	% High Client Choice (6)	% High Autonomy in Their Work (7)	% High Encroachment on Practice (8)
Rural Missouri	201	58	19	8	53	39	92	33
Springfield, MO	77	35	40	34	57	18	84	35
Chicago (total)	699	40	52	45	50	55	54	30
Corporate Cluster	151	33	62	53	60	56	44	30
Personal Plight Cluster	171	52	42	36	45	45	65	34

Source: Chicago data from Heinz and Laumann, 1982. Reprinted with permission.

concern for technical rules. The rural attorney primarily handles individual clients, whose matters usually call less for technical mastery and more for interpersonal skills. In Chicago—where entities are the typical clients—the professional skill in greatest demand is technical expertise. Again, the personal plight sector most closely approximates the rural experience, and the Springfield bar is more closely identified with that segment of the Chicago experience.

The second pair of statements, reported in column (3), taps a somewhat similar dimension to the first. It asks whether or not the attorney's practice is sufficiently technical that even an educated layperson could not really understand or prepare the documents, as opposed to a practice where a paraprofessional could be easily trained to handle many of the procedures and papers. Only 19 percent of the country lawyers considered their work to be so technical that a layperson could not be expected to understand the documents. In contrast, 52 percent of the Chicago lawyers so characterized their work, and even those in the persosnal plight cluster were far more likely to attribute such esoteric technical characteristics to their work.

The explanation for this difference again lies in client differentiation. The greater the proportion of business and corporate clientele, the greater the perception that technical skill surpassing a lay understanding is required of lawyers. It is true that much of a rural lawyer's work deals with making out wills, handling divorces, and conveying property—which is activity easily comprehended by laypersons. But the contrast in opinion between the rural and the Springfield samples is surprisingly large, given the fact that a high proporation of Springfield attorneys have predominantly individual clients. This may suggest that, despite similarities in practice patterns, lawyers in different settings come to operate out of different frames of reference.

The third pair of statements, with results shown in column (4), asks the attorneys to assess how specialized their practice is. Only 8 percent of the rural bar agreed that because their practice is so specialized, they must concentrate exclusively in that one area of practice. In contrast, 45 percent of the Chicago lawyers saw their practice in that way. The Springfield bar, as expected, fell between the two extremes. The majority of the 8 percent of rural attorneys who saw their work as highly specialized either were older attorneys who did only estate and probate work or else were trial lawyers.

The area of greatest agreement between the contrasting bars had to do with the degree of change occurring in their area of practice. As reported in column (5) of Table 2.5 more than half of the rural, Springfield, and Chicago bars agreed that "my area of practice requires a great deal of reading of legal material in order to keep abreast of new developments in the law." The Chicago personal plight sector were the least likely to so describe themselves—but only by a small (5 percent) margin. The rural attorneys were clearly sensitive to the risks entailed in being general practitioners at a time when many changes are occurring in certain fields of law. Doing all the reading required to keep them current in most of the major fields of law was seen as impossible. Some have acted to restrict their practice, even though this will cut into their earnings. Others rely on the continuing education program of the Missouri Bar to keep them current. All feel the stress of trying to be a general practitioner at a time when the requisite knowledge for such a practice is probably beyond human capacity. As one attorney expressed it, "I've joined the doctors in worrying about malpractice suits!"

As reported in column (6), attorneys in all three settings were asked whether or not they feel that, in the course of their practice, they have wide latitude in selecting which clients they will represent. Not surprisingly, Chicago lawyers were more likely to feel this way (55 percent) than rural lawyers (39 percent). Where the pool of clients is largest, not only is there more room for selectivity but the consequences of selectivity are reduced. The rural attorney has a smaller pool of potential clients to begin with, which means that being too selective may not be economically prudent. In addition, if a rejected lover is a danger anywhere, a refused client is certainly a risk in a small town where the lawyer's reputation is his primary tool for business-getting. Most of the rural lawyers admitted that it is difficult to be selective both for economic and for reputational reasons, especially in the early stages of a career. Once the reputation is well established and the income is up to a comfortable level, however, they feel freer to "prune the client load a bit."

As would be expected, there is a significant difference in the rural lawyer's perception of his autonomy as compared with that of the Chicago attorney—as shown in column (7). More than 90 percent of the country lawyers agreed that "one of the things I like about my area of practice is that I can do largely whatever I like without having someone looking over my shoulder and directing my work." Only slightly over half (54 percent) of the Chicago sample were able to describe their work in this way. No doubt, the higher the proportion of firm practice—especially large firm practice—the greater becomes the need for coordination of specialized practitioners, whose work is defined by their specialty and whose clients really belong to one of the senior partners. Large firm practice and autonomy are not likely to coexist (Heinz and Laumann, 1982:335–36, 365–73).

By contrast, the sole practitioner defines the essence of professional autonomy. He directs his own work, chooses his own clients, makes his own judgments, and earns his own rewards. What may appear somewhat surprising is that 92 percent of the rural sample did see themselves as just that autonomous when 45 percent of the rural bar are actually working in two-to-three person firms. In fact, however, two-to-three person firms in the country are essentially office-sharing arrangements and not technically "firms" as such. Then, too, many such small firms contain equal partners—which facilitates the experience of autonomy.

However, the sense of autonomy in rural practice may exceed the actual substance of autonomy. The social characteristics of small communities impose some limitations on independence from the outset. While he *can* be selective in the clients he chooses, the country lawyer probably will not be, especially in his early years. While he *can* be independent in his judgments, community standards also exert their subtle force in quite direct ways. Nonetheless, for the country lawyer, his perceived independence is his professional badge. As one attorney expressed it, "You aren't a lawyer if you aren't independent."

Finally, column (8) shows that only about a third of all the lawyers in each setting felt that "there are aspects of my professional work which are being encroached upon by other occupations." There was no significant contextual variation, which is perhaps counterintuitive. In large urban settings where CPAs abound as well as large real estate firms with their own closing departments, one might guess that attorneys would complain more about encroachment. But apparently, for the vast majority of attorneys in whatever setting, encroachment is not a major worry.

To summarize, the seven queries addressed above are presumed to be able to show that different kinds of law practice require different kinds of legal expertise and generate different kinds of perceptions of the character of the practice environment. Our primary question involves the degree to which context is responsible for these variations. Because the rural setting is a person-intensive practice environment while the metropolitan setting is an entity-intensive environment, we should expect differences in salient practice skills. As expected, rural practitioners are more likely to see their practice as calling for interpersonal skills of negotiation and advising, as opposed to calling for highly refined technical expertise. They were also far more likely to concede that laypersons could be trained to do much of the work they regularly do. Less than 10 percent felt that their work is so highly specialized that it requires them to exclude all other areas of practice. None of the foregoing is surprising when one takes the context into account. When the preponderance of clients are persons bringing predom-

Table 2.6
Law Practice Income

Law Practice Income* (in constant 1981 dollars)	% of Lawyers: Rural Missouri (n=201)	Springfield Missouri (n=77)	Chicago Total (n=724)
Below $25,000	14.5	23.6	8.4
$25,000 to 34,999	15.4	14.0	16.6
$35,000 to 49,999	23.4	17.1	23.6
$50,000 to 69,999	20.4	22.1	16.6
$70,000 to 100,000	18.5	14.3	18.0
over $100,000	8.0	9.1	16.9

Source: Chicago data are from Heinz and Laumann, 1982. Reprinted with permission.
*Chicago data collected in 1974. Transformation to 1981 dollars based on data from *National Survey of Professional, Administrative and Clerical Pay*, March 1981, by the U.S. Department of Labor which showed attorney earnings increasing 72% between 1974 and 1981.

inantly routine matters of divorce, real estate acquisition, personal injury, criminal defense, and estate issues, the requisite skills are more interpersonal than technical.

The ambivalence over the autonomy issue and the degree of discretion in choice of clients nicely summarizes the contextual impact. Entrepreneurial practice is a virtual necessity in the country, which carries with it a profound sense of independence. But in many ways, that independence is conditioned by the small environment, where it may be neither prudent nor economic to assert one's perceived independence by being excessively selective in taking clients. So an inherent tension emerges between the prize of automony and the constraints of the small community.

LAW PRACTICE INCOME

> What the boys in the cities don't know is that us country lawyers do pretty damn well.
>
> An attorney in a rural Missouri town of 8,000

Law practice income in the country is indeed comparable to law practice income in larger settings, with one major exception. As Table 2.6 indicates, a higher proportion of big city attorneys will show earnings in the very top category. Beyond that distinction, the rural and urban proportions earning middle-range salaries are quite equivalent.

There is an interesting contrast between the rural bar and the Springfield bar. The proportion of lawyers in the lowest category of earnings is higher in Spring-

Table 2.7
Law Income, by Client Type

Practice Settings	N	Mean % of Income From Business Clients	Mean % of Income From Major Corporate Clients
Rural Missouri	201	34	8
Springfield, Missouri	77	52	24
Chicago (Total)	699	58	35
Corporate Cluster	151	92	62
Personal Plight Cluster	171	23	10

Source: Chicago data are from Heinz and Laumann, 1982. Reprinted with permission.

field than in rural areas. This appears to be an artifact of the more highly developed firm-practice pattern in Springfield. The proportion of firm associates (beginning lawyers hired at a set salary) in the Springfield sample was 19.5 percent. By contrast, the rural sample contained only 4 percent who worked as associates. Assuming the randomness of the sample was not compromised, this suggests that there is nearly five times the likelihood to practice as an associate in a mid-size urban setting as there is in the country setting. This is understandable given the fact that, the more urban the setting, the greater the likelihood of firm practice—which relies on associates.

With very few firms of any size in country practice, the small proportion of associates there is not surprising. But it does point up a contextual difference that helps to explain the higher proportion of lower incomes in Springfield. Many times, associates' salaries are relatively low even as compared to the earnings of junior partners. In the country, on the other hand, earnings represent the relative effectiveness of the practitioner's entrepreneurial skills. The beginning entrepreneur is not—by definition—locked into a low salary, as is the case with a beginning associate. He simply gets what he earns, and apparently he can usually earn more than an associate can get.

The most significant variable that explains earning differentials in the rural bar is years in practice. Lawyers in practice for 15 years earned more than twice as much as lawyers in practice for less than 5 years.

As expected, the larger the setting, the greater the proportion of law earnings coming from business clients as opposed to individual clients with personal matters. Table 2.7 shows this monotonic relationship. Rural lawyers derive only about one-third of their income from business clients while members of the Chicago bar derive 58 percent of their income from such clients.

For rural lawyers, while they do handle a wide variety of matters, it is also clear that their bread and butter comes from only three areas of practice: estate, domestic, and negligence or personal injury practice. As Table 2.8 indicates, more than two-thirds of the entire rural sample indicated that either estate practice, domestic relations, or negligence practice provided the largest proportion of their

Table 2.8
Practice Areas Producing Highest Proportion of Income (% of attorneys)

Practice Area	Highest Proportion of Income		Second Highest Proportion of Income		Third Highest Proportion of Income		Overall Rank of Practice Areas as Source of Income	
	Rural	Urban	Rural	Urban	Rural	Urban	Rural	Urban
Estate	27.9	10.4	16.9	13.0	12.4	7.8	1	3
Domestic	19.4	5.6	26.9	9.1	19.4	39.0	2	2
Negligence	21.4	32.5	12.9	20.8	10.9	5.2	3	1
Real Estate	8.0	3.9	13.5	7.8	16.4	7.8	4	6
Criminal Defense	6.0	5.2	7.5	2.6	11.4	2.6	5	10
General Corporate	1.0	9.1	4.0	13.0	2.5	2.6	9	4
Commercial, Contracts	1.5	7.8	2.5	10.4	3.0	7.8	10	5

law income. These areas were also a primary source of income for the Springfield bar, but only for about 48 percent of the sample. Corporate practice—even in the smaller urban setting—was the fourth ranked area for law practice income, while in the country it ranked no higher than ninth.

Income in the country, while it is roughly equivalent to income in more urban settings except at the highest ranges, represents a very different dollar/client ratio. If we take an average lawyer earning $60,000 in rural practice and spread that income out over the median number of clients (350), it yields an average net income of about $171 per client. The Chicago sample, on the other hand—with a median client load of only 35—reflects $1,714 net income per client. The value of such a computation lies only in suggesting that smaller settings tend to generate income by presenting the attorney with a large number of smaller matters while the more metropolitan area is characterized by a relatively small number of larger matters.

SUMMARY

The primary argument advanced here is that there is an ecology of law practice. The roots of the practice of law are less attached to the doctrinal areas learned in professional school than they are to the distinguishing characteristics of the containing community where the practice occurs. This is what makes the legal profession an externally determined social system. It takes its shape from the contours of the context as opposed to the autonomous content of its technical and doctrinal principles. Thus it resonates largely to its environment and displays the impact of external forces.

A variety of analogies are suggested. The profession mirrors its containing community in the ethno-religious makeup of the bar. Heterogeneous communities generate heterogeneous bars. The scale of practice mimics the scale of enterprise in the containing community. The bureaucratically organized firm is commonplace in the large-scale economic setting. The entrepreneurial practice mode is found in the smaller settings where entrepreneurship is the mode. There is a symmetry between community actors and clients, as well. In large settings where entities are the powerful actors, they are also the modal clients. In smaller settings where persons are the primary actors, they are also the primary clients. The profile of the rural bar stands in stark contrast to the profile of the metropolitan bar. The contrasts appear to mirror ecological or environmental differences.

3

THE IMPACT OF COMMUNITY SIZE ON PROFESSIONAL STRATIFICATION

> The vast majority of people in smaller towns think of themselves as just "plain folk." And most of them are. Sure, there are a few big operators around but they'll never keep a country lawyer in business. So I've never tried to corner the big client market. There's not enough there to keep you. I can show up in town in my overalls and be "plain folk" with the rest and have a good law practice.
>
> A Missouri lawyer
> in a town of 6,000

The hallmark of the practicing bar in metropolitan settings is its hierarchy. Behind the vast diversity of urban practice stands a steep and rigid system of social stratification that parcels out clients, wealth, power, and professional status in a very systematic way (Ladinsky, 1963; Carlin, 1966; Heinz and Laumann, 1982:385).

The elite typically practice in large firms while the lowest stratum practices alone or in small firms. The gulf that separates the two is immense. Their incomes are different. Members of the elite bar represent the most affluent and prestigious clients. They also move among the highest levels of the judiciary and have contact with the highest levels of government. Members of the lower stratum bar—on the other hand—have lower incomes and represent less affluent, less prestigious, and less powerful clients. Lower status attorneys are also more typically found working within the lowest levels of the court system and interacting with lower status government officials. Contact between lawyers in the differing strata is limited—exacerbating the problems of hierarchy.

This systematic differentiation within the metropolitan bar has been growing over the years. The Chicago bar, for example, has become so steeply and rigidly stratified that Heinz and Laumann concluded there are two legal professions in that city—"one recruited from more privileged origins and the other from less prestigious backgrounds. . . . The first kind of lawyer serves corporate clients that are quite wealthy and powerful, and the other serves individuals and small businesses that are far less powerful" (1982:385). This fragmentation of the legal profession into two virtually independent hemispheres that constitute two virtually separate occupational groups suggests "a corresponding stratification of law into two systems of justice, separate and unequal" (Heinz and Laumann, 1982:385). The inference is that prestigious corporate clients are the beneficiaries of the best legal talent available while individual clients and small businesses are served by a residual bar.

But the ramifications of professional stratification do not stop at generating two separate but unequal systems of justice. Research in the New York City bar suggests that lawyers' adherence to ethical norms are, in part, a function of their placement in the stratification system (Carlin, 1966). Carlin argues that "many of the factors that serve to mark and separate the various strata are the very factors that determine the kinds of ethical controls to which lawyers are exposed in their practice" (1966:23). The effect of this structuring of ethical conduct is to put individual clients and small businesses at greater risk. Lower status lawyers typically deal with cases and situations in which the opportunity, the pressure, and the vulnerability to ethical violation is maximized.

In metropolitan settings the single most significant variable affecting the structure and practice characteristics of the legal profession is this stratification of the bar. It fragments the profession, undermines the integrity of the justice system, discriminates against less prestigious clientele, and demoralizes practitioners who are relegated to the periphery of professional practice.

THE ROLE OF COMMUNITY SIZE

Before the bar can become stratified and acquire the hierarchical qualities described earlier, a variety of factors must be present. These are clearly seen in the metropolitan bar. First, there must be a sufficiently heterogeneous mix of clients within a sufficiently large population to permit the opportunity for focusing practice more or less exclusively on a single class of clients or interests. This division of labor within the bar tends to institutionalize itself within the framework of firm size. The largest clients, such as corporations, typically have a broad range of legal concerns that require a variety of highly skilled specialists. This need becomes the source of "institutional" law practice (Wells, 1964), with scores of attorneys collaborating on matters dealing with a few large clients.

Under these conditions law practice becomes bureaucratized (Nelson, 1983), which contributes to the stratifying process.

This specialization in metropolitan settings is dictated more by client needs than by cognitive or substantive coherence (Laumann and Heinz, 1977). Thus instead of exclusive practice in one substantive field of law, metropolitan settings tend to generate patterns of "co-practice" in which firms develop practice patterns that are tied to client characteristics rather than to the traditional substantive divisions of law. Such "client-driven" differentiation within law practice is a central feature of the Chicago bar (Heinz and Laumann, 1982:ch. 2).

Second, professional stratification appears to be facilitated by significant heterogeneity within the bar. All the studies of the metropolitan bar (Carlin, 1966:ch. 2; Heinz and Laumann, 1982:ch. 3; Ladinsky, 1963; Zemans and Rosenblum, 1981:chs. 3, 5) indicate that ethno-religious differences among lawyers are strongly associated with differences in career patterns. White, Anglo-Saxon, Protestant backgrounds typically attend the best law schools and are more likely to get positions in the larger firms that do work for prestigious clients. Lawyers from ethnic backgrounds tend to go to less prestigious law schools and appear to compete less well for positions in leading firms. The distribution of opportunity in the bar reflects the distributive patterns in the larger community. In cities where there are ethno-religious minorities there tends to be an ethnic bar.

Third, when the practicing bar becomes diverse enough to be unambiguously associated with classes of clients that already possess differing statuses in the community, the process of differentiation becomes hierarchicalized. The horizontal process of differentiation becomes verticalized into a system of hierarchy. Normative meanings are attached to practice types. The value system within the profession bestows on certain practice specialties a status not granted to others (Abbott, 1981). Moreover, the value system of the larger society impinges on the more or less discrete division of labor within the bar and identifies certain classes of clients as more prestigious than others. The status and power of persons or organizations in the larger society come to reflect positively or negatively on the practitioner who represents them (Heinz and Laumann, 1982:ch. 5). If it is feasible to build an exclusive practice in which essentially one class of clients is served, the practitioner is likely to acquire a relatively unambiguous professional status—a status that mirrors the social esteem of his or her clients.

Fourth and finally, the inequalities generated by ethnic background, law school background, firm size, and client differences become structured and institutionalized in a variety of ways. For example, both Carlin (1966:35) and Heinz and Laumann (1982:ch. 8) document the existence of different professional associations within the same metropolitan communities. These differing local bars are made up of differing strata within the local profession and pursue differing political agendas commensurate with their differing interests. There is also a "geography" of professional practice in metropolitan communities. Elite practitioners locate on Wall Street in New York and on LaSalle Street in Chicago.

Lower strata lawyers disperse themselves into the areas where their clients are most likely to be found, which ultimately includes ethnic neighborhoods.

Thus the metropolitan community with its large and heterogeneous population, its already existing systems of power and status, its vast contrasts of wealth, and its highly differentiated business and residential locations is ideally suited to generating a stratified bar.

This connection between community size and professional stratification was documented by Joel Handler (1967) in his study of the Prairie City, Illinois bar. Handler was exploring the impact of community size on lawyers' ethics by comparing data from his middle-size (population 90,000) midwestern community with Carlin's (1966) data from the New York City bar. While he found differences among the Prairie City lawyers in terms of clients, practice characteristics, and income, these differences were offset by the similarities: mixed clientele, homogeneous lawyer backgrounds, a lack of specialization, a single local bar association, and a great deal of professional and social contact among practitioners. The centrifugal forces were not so strong as the centripetal forces. Consequently, the Prairie City bar retained a striking homogeneity in contrast to the steeply stratified New York City bar.

THE CASE OF THE RURAL BAR

Our data from practitioners in smaller towns further test the proposition that community size is a primary variable affecting the extent of professional stratification. In a community with as few as three or four lawyers, there is not going to be a stratified bar. There may be some differences in income and client characteristics, but there simply are not enough lawyers to create discrete strata. On these grounds alone the inquiry into the issue of stratification in the rural bar may seem misplaced. Nonetheless there are differences among practitioners across the small settings and it is instructive to examine the extent to which these differences become structured.

Making a tour of the law offices in metropolitan settings, one can immediately sense the difference between practitioners. Some offices are in elite downtown locations—each firm spread over many floors of the high-rise office buildings. The entrance may be marked by exquisite walnut paneling with gold lettering announcing the firm name. Inside are thick carpets, period furniture, art objects, *Baron's*, and the *Atlantic Monthly*. By contrast, other practitioners' offices are located in neighborhood business areas. The building may be shared by a tailor, a cleaning establishment, and a collection agency. The entry door is probably painted. The office interior walls are decorated with calendars. The floor is linoleum tile. A lamp table has a stack of *People*, *Reader's Digest*, and *Sports Illustrated* magazines. These are some of the visible reminders of the differing "hemispheres of practice" in large settings.

To be sure, rural attorneys are not all cut from the same cloth. They, too, are distinguishable. On occasion they convey strikingly different images even in the same town. In one community of 9,000, two contrasting practice settings illustrate the variety that can be found. One firm with five lawyers is located away from downtown in a residential setting dominated by large gracious Victorian homes. The firm has remodeled one of the two-story homes into an elegant office. Shaded, relaxed, and manicured, the setting appeals to persons of taste. Entering the office, one is confronted with period living room furniture and a wall full of academic credentials and various awards. The *Wall Street Journal* lies on the coffee table along with a recent issue of *Harper's*. The office has modern word processing equipment and a substantial library, and the walls contain paintings of the family including a banker-lawyer who founded the firm many years ago. You would expect persons in three-piece suits to come and go.

Three blocks away, just off Main Street, is a cinder block one-story law office. Only street parking is available. A glass door opens into a well-lighted office where a middle-age receptionist who is also the secretary sits at a typewriter. This sole practitioner's office is Spartan. There is a desk, desk chair, and three chairs for clients. A modest set of bookcases contains the office library. On the walls are family pictures, a graduation invitation, a wedding invitation, and several photos of grandchildren. The low-key lawyer sitting in shirt sleeves behind his desk has a relaxed manner. He talks about the town, its people, their problems, and his satisfaction with his practice. He remarks, "Lawyers are for people. I've helped a lot of people over the years. I can't think of anything else I'd rather do." On the way out, one notices a pregnant girl and an older man in bib overalls waiting in the office.

The differences between the two law firms are clearly visible. And there are some differences in their clients. But the differences are more apparent than real. The emulation of elite firm practice is observed occasionally in small towns; but, by and large, there is more that make rural practitioners similar than dissimilar.

INCOME: THE MEASURE OF STATUS AND SUCCESS

The most significant differentiating factor among rural practitioners is income. In our study, for the previous year (1981), full-time law practice produced incomes under $20,000 for some, while others indicated incomes over $100,000 (see Table 3.1).

Status for the entrepreneurial practitioner is conceived of essentially in material terms. Because sole practice and small firms are the norm in small settings, the opportunity to acquire status by gaining partnership in a prestigious firm is unavailable. While client differences are present in smaller towns, I found no practitioners who claimed to represent corporate or other high-status clients exclusively. Therefore the most accessible means of lawyer differentiation in the country is income. It is the single most powerful centrifugal force within the rural bar. But as subsequent data will show, the other factors associated with

Table 3.1
Law Practice Income, 1981, Rural Lawyers in Missouri

Income	% of Rural Sample
under $10,000	1.5
$10 - $14,999	2.0
$15 - $19,999	4.0
$20 - $29,999	15.4
$30 - $39,999	13.9
$40 - $49,999	16.4
$50 - $59,999	10.0
$60 - $69,999	10.4
$70 - $79,999	5.5
$80 - $89,999	6.0
$90 - $99,999	7.0
$100,000 or more	8.0
	100.0%

Table 3.2
Cross-tabulation of Community Size, by Law Practice Income

Size of Community in which law practice occurs	under $30,000 (n=46)	$30,000 to $59,999 (n=81)	$60,000 to $99,000 (n=58)	over $100,000 (n=16)	Row Total
under 1000 (n=23)	9	17	7	6	11.4
1000-2499 (n=39)	28	21	12	12	19.4
2500-4999 (n=50)	24	26	24	25	24.9
5000-9999 (n=51)	13	24	35	38	25.4
Column Totals	22.9	40.3	28.9	8.0	100.0

income differences are so diffuse as to make it difficult to discern any meaningful strata.

We selected a range of variables that our theoretical model suggested might be associated with lawyer earnings. These included community size, practice setting, client characteristics, practice areas, and—finally—years in practice.

As one might expect, community size appears to be positively related to income, but not unambiguously so (see Table 3.2). Attorneys in towns of less than 1,000 are disproportionately represented in the lower income brackets while attorneys in towns with a population of 5,000 to 9,999 are most likely to have incomes in the two highest brackets. The largest settings in our study (10,000–20,000) appeared to have rather equal representation in each income category and thus did not sustain the expected relationship of income to community size. However, we would assume that with an increase in community size there will be an absolute increase in business clients. Therefore it is not surprising to find a relationship (albeit weak) between the size of the town and the size of the income.

Table 3.3
Firm Size, by Law Practice Income (Rural Missouri Sample)

	% of Lawyers Earning				
Practice Setting	Under $30,000 (n=46)	$30,000 to $59,999 (n=81)	$60,000 to $99,999 (n=58)	Over $100,000 (n=16)	Row Total
Solo (n=86)	48	43	41	31	42.8
Firm (2-3) (n=90)	46	48	40	44	44.8
Firm (4-5) (n=20)	6	9	12	19	10.0
Firm (6-8) (n=2)	0	0	3	0	1.0
Firm (9-12) (n=3)	0	0	3	6	1.5
	100	100	100	100	100.0

Percentages may vary from 100 due to rounding.

The data in Table 3.3 also indicate that the attorneys in larger firms in the countryside are more likely to have higher earnings. The cell sizes of firms of from six to eight and nine to twelve attorneys are so small that valid conclusions cannot be drawn; but it does appear that, in general, attorneys in larger firms are more likely to achieve higher incomes than those practicing solo. Again, the relationship here is similar to what is generally the case in metropolitan areas, but not nearly so well developed. The relationship of firm size to income did not achieve statistical significance and therefore, while the trend is in the expected direction, it could also be attributed to chance.

CLIENTELE AND INCOME

The data in Table 3.4 suggest that there is a statistically significant relationship between client types served and law practice income. While—again—the cell size is quite small, it does appear that lawyers whose earnings are derived primarily from clients other than individuals are more likely to have higher incomes than those who receive the bulk (more than 75 percent) of their incomes from personal matters. It is important to note, however, that a significant proportion (35 percent) of attorneys whose income was 75 percent or more derived from personal matters still managed to achieve law earnings of more than $60,000.

The data in Table 3.4 also suggest that those who can get a large proportion of their income from major corporations are also more likely to have higher total practice earnings. While more than 86 percent of the rural sample derived 10 percent or less of their income from major corporations, the 14 percent who did have significant corporate practice (25 percent or more) were much more likely to achieve high incomes. Again, this finding is consistent with the trends located in larger settings. The difference is that the proportion of lawyers enjoying a

Table 3.4
Sources of Law Practice Income, by Total Earnings (Rural Missouri Sample)

	% of Attorneys Earnings				
Source of Law Income	Under $30,000	$30,000 to $59,999	$60,000 to $99,999	Over $100,000	Row Total
Work, for Individual Clients					
-produced 30% or less (n=10)	0	0	12	19	5.0
-produced 40%-75% (n=138)	65	78	62	56	68.7
-produced over 75% (n=53)	35	22	26	25	26.4
	100	100	100	100	100.0
Column Total	22.9	40.3	28.9	8.0	100.0
			Sig = .0013		
Business Client Income					
From Major Corporations					
-produced 10% or less (n=174)	94	91	79	69	86.6
-produced 15%-45% (n=10)	4	6	3	6	5.0
-produced 50% or more (n=17)	2	3	17	25	8.5
	100	100	100	100	100.0
			Sig = .0042		

Percentages may vary from 100 due to rounding.

substantial corporate practice in rural settings is very small. The data indicate that only 4.5 percent of the rural sample had 25 percent or more of their time invested in corporate practice. More than 62 percent had less than 5 percent of their practice in corporate matters.

Country lawyers are fundamentally practitioners with very mixed clientele. Virtually all have individual clients in addition to business and corporate clients. Only 2.5 percent have fewer than 25 percent of their total client load in the form of individuals with personal matters. Seventy percent indicate that at least three-fourths of their clients are persons rather than business or corporate entities. But individual clients differ in terms of their socioeconomic status. The data in Table 3.5 suggest the expected: The higher the proportion of individual clients who come from professional-managerial backgrounds, the more likely is the attorney to have a higher income. Those whose individual clients are disproportionately from blue-collar backgrounds are less likely to be included in the high-income categories. Again, this is consistent with our expectations. However, only in the case of the professional-managerial client group did the relationship achieve statistical significance.

Using a similar technique of evaluating the status of business clients, Table 3.5 further indicates that those attorneys whose largest source of business clients is corporations are those most likely to achieve high incomes. While only 9 percent of the rural sample reported corporations as the largest source of their business clients, those 9 percent accounted for one-fourth of all who earned $100,000 a year or more. On the other hand, nearly half of the rural sample reported that their largest source of business clients was small businesses, but

Table 3.5
Client Types, by Law Income

Client Characteristics	Rural Missouri Sample % of Lawyers Earning Under $30,000 (n=46)	$30,000 to $59,999 (n=81)	$60,000 to $99,999 (n=58)	Over $100,000 (n=16)	Row Total
Professional-Managerial					
-10% or less (n=109)	74	59	40	25	54.2
-15-25% (n=65)	22	32	38	44	32.3
-30% or more (n=27)	4	9	22	31	13.4
	100	100	100	100	100%
		Sig. = .0009			
Blue Collar					
-25% or less (n=38)	20	11	26	31	18.9
-30-50% (n=87)	33	51	43	38	43.3
-over 50% (n=76)	48	38	31	31	37.8
	100	100	100	100	100%
		Sig. = .1315			
Largest Source of Business Clients					
-major corporation (n=18)	2	4	17	25	9.0
-medium size business (n=43)	22	20	22	25	21.4
-small business (n=98)	48	53	47	38	48.8
-large scale farming (n=14)	0	8	10	6	7.0
-other (n=28)	28	15	3	6	13.9
	100	100	100	100	100%
		Sig. = .0017			

that half constituted only 38 percent of those whose incomes topped $100,000 in 1981.

While these findings about client differences are generally in the expected direction and tend to reflect the patterns found more explicitly in the metropolitan bar, there are sufficient ambiguities to warrant caution in suggesting that the rural and metropolitan bars experience the same client/income structuring.

THE IMPACT OF SUBSTANTIVE PRACTICE AREAS ON INCOME

It is generally thought that practice for business and corporate entities is more remunerative than practice for persons. Therefore it might be assumed that

Table 3.6
Practice Areas, by Law Income

	Rural Missouri Sample % of Lawyers Earning			
Practice Areas	Under $30,000	$30,000 to $59,999	$60,000 to $99,999	Over $100,000
Agriculture				
-under 5% of practice (n=150)	78	75	71	75
-over 5% of practice (n=51)	22	25	29	25
Administrative Law*				
-under 5% (n=170)	89	86	88	50
-over 5% (n=31)	11	14	12	50
Banking				
-under 5% (n=107)	65	54	43	50
-over 5% (n=94)	35	46	57	50
Civil Rights and Liberties				
-under 5% (n=192)	98	96	91	100
-over 5% (n=9)	2	4	9	0
Collections*				
-under 5% (n=120)	44	54	72	88
-over 5% (n=81)	56	46	28	12
Commercial and Contract*				
-under 5% (n=127)	78	69	47	50
-over 5% (n=74)	22	31	53	50
Criminal Defense				
-under 5% (n=109)	61	56	45	63
-over 5% (n=92)	39	44	55	37
Criminal Prosecution				
-under 5% (n=176)	83	85	95	88
-over 5% (n=25)	17	15	5	12
Domestic				
-under 5% (n=25)	11	9	19	12
-over 5% (n=176)	89	91	81	88
Environmental*				
-under 5% (n=198)	100	100	98	88
-over 5% (n=3)	0	0	2	12
Estimate				
-under 5% (n=41)	33	12	21	25
-over 5% (n=160)	67	88	79	75

Practice Areas	Under $30,000	Rural Missouri Sample % of Lawyers Earning $30,000 to $59,999	$60,000 to $99,999	Over $100,000
General Corporate*				
-under 5% (n=126)	74	65	57	38
-over 5% (n=75)	26	35	43	62
General Litigation*				
-under 5% (n=160)	87	95	62	44
-over 5% (n=41)	13	5	38	56
General Personal				
-under 5% (n=140)	57	72	79	63
-over 5% (n=61)	43	28	21	37
Municipal				
-under 5% (n=143)	74	63	81	69
-over 5% (n=58)	26	37	19	31
Negligence (defendant)*				
-under 5% (n=144)	78	82	62	38
-over 5% (n=57)	22	18	38	62
Negligence (plaintiff)*				
-under 5% (n=65)	44	37	22	13
-over 5% (n=136)	56	63	78	87
Real Estate (commercial)				
-under 5% (n=110)	61	62	45	38
-over 5% (n=91)	39	38	55	62
Real Estate (residential)				
-under 5% (n=78)	33	36	41	63
-over 5% (n=123)	67	64	59	37
Taxation (corporate)				
-under 5% (n=188)	98	97	86	94
-over 5% (n=13)	2	3	14	6
Taxation (personal)				
-under 5% (n=159)	80	78	79	81
-over 5% (n=42)	20	22	21	19

*Significant at .05 or less

lawyers withamount of criminal defense work would show significantly lower earnings than their colleagues who do generally corporate work. The data in Table 3.6 explore this relationship between income and substantive area.

Thirteen of the twenty-one substantive areas of practice listed in Table 3.6 fail to show any significant relationship between area of practice and lawyer income. Our data compare lawyers who had less than 5 percent of their practice in a particular substantive area with those who had more than 5 percent. Because of the generality of rural practice, the 5 percent cutoff seemed to separate those with relatively little work in an area from those with an appreciable amount.

Collections showed a predictable relationship. Long considered a residual practice area in urban settings, even country lawyers who devote more than 5 percent of their practice to collecting delinquent accounts for businesses are unlikely to enjoy high incomes.

The other practice areas that had a statistically significant relationship with lawyer income include administrative law, commercial and contract work, general corporate practice, general litigation, and negligence practice (both defendant and plaintiff). It is of interest to note that these practice areas tend to include both individual client matters and business and corporate matters. Negligence (plaintiff) practice is primarily representing persons against insurance companies or other corporate entities. General litigation in the country is disproportionately related to individual client problems. Commercial and contract practice as well as general corporate practice are entity related rather than individual related. There appears again to be a rather ambiguous relationship between substantive areas of practice and lawyer income. Business and corporate practice are not uniformly the source of high income among country practitioners.

SENIORITY AND INCOME

Rural lawyers uniformly suggested that the road to high income in a country practice is perseverance. As one attorney in a town of 6,000 expressed it,

> There's no short cut to good earnings in the country. You pay your dues and bide your time. If you hang in there long enough you'll probably make a damn good living.

The data in Table 3.7 tend to support his observation. Lawyers in practice for less than five years are disproportionately located in the lower income categories. Lawyers who had practiced between 16 and 35 years represent only 35 percent of the sample, but they constitute nearly two-thirds of the group who earned more than $100,000 in 1981. The most senior group (36 or more years in practice) appear to reflect a retirement pattern, with none showing incomes in the highest category. But the size of that group ($N = 13$) is too small to warrant generalizing.

From a variety of cross-tabulations, we identified six variables that appear to be significantly related to higher earnings for rural lawyers. They include size

Table 3.7
Years in Practice, by Law Income (Rural Missouri Sample)

	% of Lawyers Earning				
Years in Practice	Under $30,000	$30,000 to $59,999	$60,000 to $99,999	Over $100,000	Row Total
5 years or less (n=28)	37	12	2	0	13.9
6-15 years (n=89)	35	53	41	38	44.3
16-35 years (n=71)	20	30	48	62	35.3
Over 35 years (n=13)	9	5	9	0	6.5
					100

Sig. = .0001

of community; years in practice; proportion of practice in estate work, corporate work, and civil litigation; and client volume. Further analysis indicates that, of all these variables, the number of years in practice is most significantly associated with high income—accounting for 34 percent of the variance.

TIME AND THE REFINEMENT OF PRACTICE

Country lawyers uniformly report a two-pronged strategy for achieving a good income—the mark of entrepreneurial success. The first strategy involves patience and perseverence. The second involves pruning the practice.

The pruning process begins with one of the imperatives of entrepreneurial endeavor: the need to earn a living while building a practice. In the early years of practice, this involves doing virtually whatever presents itself to be done. There will be lots of divorce work, some collection work, some criminal defense work, making out wills, handling real estate transactions, doing personal taxes, some small business matters and bankruptcies—nearly anything that will create income and/or lead to establishing client connections. Client volume is the name of the game in the early years.

Clearly, some legal matters are more remunerative than others. Some clients are more desirable than others. Within the limitations of the local environment, country lawyers try to refine their practices once they have established themselves in the community. This pruning process involves referring less desirable matters to younger attorneys or indicating to prospective clients that you "don't do bankruptcies."

But the refining process is difficult. First of all, there is the promise of future business to worry about. You do not tell a prospective client in a small town that you "just don't handle divorce cases." As one attorney expressed it,

I hate to get involved in divorce work. It's messy. The cases never end. Four years after the decree you are still trying to settle quarrels over visitation and child support. And for the hours spent they don't pay well. But you can't just say "no" to them. Someday they may have a damage suit or the like and you want them to be sure to come back. So it's not easy to avoid undesirable work even when you can afford to.

Then there is the matter of reputation. The small town attorney prospers or fails on the strength of his reputation throughout the community. The process of building reputation is arduous, and protecting it is a career-long enterprise. Central to the country lawyer's reputation is his willingness and capacity to help. He is seen by many in the community—simplistically—as a helper for all seasons. It can be fatal to betray the helper image. One attorney who had successfully pruned his practice said,

It has taken me years to be able to avoid criminal cases. I was prosecuting attorney in this county once and got a reputation for being good in court. I guess they assumed that if I was good as prosecutor I would be good as a criminal defense lawyer as well. My career started down that path without my wishing it. I finally just stopped taking criminal cases, but I've paid a price. There's some other kinds of law work I'd rather not do but still find myself weighing the options and asking what it will cost me if I pruned out divorce work or collections. There's only so much pruning you can do in the country without risking your whole practice.

Many of the long-established attorneys in rural settings see probate work as the ultimate practice. To be able to refine the practice until a substantial part of it is devoted to probate work is, in the words of one attorney, "to enter the land of milk and honey."

BACKGROUND CHARACTERISTICS OF THE RURAL BAR

The data in Chapter 2 portray the rural bar as strikingly homogeneous in comparison with the metropolitan bar. In Chicago, Heinz and Laumann (1982:448) found vast differences in the social backgrounds of practitioners. Only 23 percent were classified as "mixed and American practitioners." The remainder were from a variety of ethnic backgrounds including Southern and Eastern European, Northern and Western European, British, Irish, and African Americans. They were religiously diverse as well. Thirty-three percent identified themselves as Jewish; 30 percent, as Catholic; 13 percent, as Type I Protestants (Congregational, Presbyterian, Episcopal, United Church of Christ); 12 percent, as Type II Protestants (Protestants other than Type I); and 12 percent, with no religious identification. This ethno-religious diversity in the bar is a microcosm of the larger metropolitan community. It also contributes to the stratification of the urban bar.

The rural bar, by contrast, was ethnically homogeneous. There were no first-generation immigrants in the sample. While their origins were all traceable to either the British Isles or to Northern and Western European countries, the families of the country lawyers had been in the United States for several generations and they considered themselves "Americans." There were no black attorneys and no Jewish attorneys. More than 83 percent identified themselves as Protestant; 14 percent, as Catholic; and only 3 percent, as having no religious affiliation. Again, the essential homogeneity of background of the rural attorneys was a reflection of the homogeneous character of the rural population from which they were drawn.

The ethnic diversity of the metropolitan bar generates a further source of differentiation within its ranks. The training of city attorneys is received at a wide range of schools. Heinz and Laumann (1982:445) identified four classifications of law schools ranging from "elite" (Chicago, Columbia, Harvard, Michigan, Stanford, and Yale), "prestige" (Berkeley, Cornell, Georgetown, New York University, Northwestern, Pennsylvania, Virginia, and Wisconsin), and "regional" (all schools not included in the prestige and elite categories except local Chicago schools), to "local" (DePaul, Chicago Kent, Lolyola, and John Marshall). Lawyers from the ethnic backgrounds were much more likely to be educated in the local schools. Forty-five percent of the Chicago bar were educated in local law schools, while prestige schools trained 17 percent of the Chicago bar. Regional schools trained 16 percent.

Again the rural sample contrasts significantly with the heterogeneity of the metropolitan bar. More than 77 percent attended the University of Missouri law schools in Columbia and in Kansas City. Another 12 percent attended either Washington University or St. Louis University. Only one lawyer attended an elite school. The remaining 10 percent attended a variety of regional schools.

CONCLUSION

In stark contrast to the metropolitan bar—which is rigidly stratified, producing multiple professions of law—the rural bar is strikingly homogeneous. Internal sources of fragmentation are relatively absent, and rural practitioners tend to experience themselves as a cohesive community.

While the tendency toward hierarchy is present in all social systems, the rural bar is deterred in developing significant divisions within its ranks. First, the smaller context means there is not a sufficiently heterogeneous pool of clients within a sufficiently large population to permit extensive specialization of practice. This is reflected in the modest size of rural law firms. Eighty-eight percent of all the attorneys in our sample were practicing either alone or in firms with one or two other attorneys. Only 2.5 percent practiced in firms with more than five lawyers. In rural settings the critical mass of similar clients necessary to support institutional practice is simply not present.

Second, the rural bar is homogeneous in background, and it serves a population that is essentially homogeneous. Ethnic, racial, and significant religious diversity are notably absent among country practitioners. They practice in communities of similar character. Again, an important precondition for professional fragmentation and stratification is missing in the rural setting.

Third, while there is a continuing effort on the part of individuals within the rural bar to refine their practice, virtually all rural lawyers have a mix of clientele that precludes exclusive identification with one class of interests or client types. There are some (less than 5 percent) who do extensive work for insurance companies in negligence cases, but the vast majority who have spent many years in refining their practices still serve a broad range of client types and substantive problems.

Then there is the egalitarian ethos of the rural community. Not that everyone is equal—but there is a sentiment that everyone belongs to the community of ordinary folk. To emphatically and publicly push for preeminence would be to violate the normative order in many towns.

In contrast to large settings where client interests are so different that multiple professional associations are organized to advance differing sets of interests, the rural bar is only loosely organized. County or judicial circuit bars exist but they do not play a critical role. The primary differentiation recognized by rural attorneys is the difference between big-city practice and country practice. In metropolitan settings, members of differing bar associations seldom interact with each other, and the social distance between them is considerable (Carlin, 1966:34). In rural settings, all country lawyers are acquainted with each other and have ongoing interactions virtually on a day-to-day basis. There is no significant social distance between them. The conditions of practice in a small town make collegiality a necessity, and therefore centripetal forces tend to override the centrifugal forces that are present.

Finally, the geography of the small town promotes collegiality and communication. Most lawyers are located on Main Street or within a few blocks of the courthouse. There is no opportunity to distinguish between downtown practice and neighborhood practice, as there is in larger settings.

The rural bar does reflect modest differentiation—most notably, in income. But it is not a stratified bar. In contrast to Chicago, there is one legal profession in the country. Its practitioners are recruited from essentially homogeneous backgrounds and have strikingly similar educational experiences. They also have quite similar client mixes, running the gamut from community notables to just plain folk. This homogeneity within the profession tends to maintain a cohesiveness within the law. There is essentially one system of justice in the country. But, for the larger profession itself, country practice represents an additional source of fragmentation. To the "hemispheres of practice" within the metropolitan setting must be added the "community of practice" found in rural settings.

An additional way of examining this issue is to extract from the metropolitan bar the segment that most nearly approximates in client characteristics and in case load the rural bar and see if community context alters those commonalities to produce two distinctively different professions. To that task we turn our attention next.

4

ENTREPRENEURIAL PRACTICE: A TALE OF TWO SETTINGS

Perhaps the strongest evidence of the impact of community context on the conduct of professional practice can be seen in comparing a common practice style in two contrasting settings. We have argued that the bar is an externally determined social system, taking its shape from the scale and character of the local institutions into which its roots are deeply thrust. In the last chapter we documented how large-scale, diverse, highly stratified metropolitan settings tend to generate a highly fragmented and stratified legal profession in which institutional or firm practice predominates and private entrepreneurial effort constitutes a residual practice type.

Our data show that smaller settings generate primarily private or entrepreneurial practice, along with very limited examples of institutional or large firm practice. The fact that both settings generate a common form of practice (entrepreneurial) provides an opportunity to examine this form under radically differing contexts. First, however, we must distinguish between "institutional" and "entrepreneurial" practices.

THE ENTREPRENEURIAL PRACTITIONER

Dan Lortie (1960) has suggested that law careers can be described as either "institutional" or "entrepreneurial." The institutional career is typically developed within a large law firm, where beginning lawyers start as employee-apprentices. They have no clients of their own. They work under the direction of more senior members of the firm. Typically they practice in a narrowly specialized area and develop a rather focused expertise. Their early years constitute a probationary period under the watchful scrutiny of more senior partners. The prize to be won is partnership. The crucial relationships in the institutional career are thus with colleagues. The latter supply the clients, delegate the work, and control the rewards of status, income, and—ultimately—partnership. As an institutional practitioner, the attorney sacrifices autonomy for security. His or her career is propelled more by sponsorship than by enterprise. The symbols of success tend to be technical recognition and hierarchical placement in the bureaucracy of the firm.

In urban settings the institutional career stands at the core of the profession. It is a career with impressive cases; prestigious, powerful, and wealthy clients; and high-status colleagues. It is the norm for urban law—a practice form that is highly articulated with the contours of corporate life.

On the other hand, the entrepreneurial career is an exercise in enterprise, not apprenticeship or probation. The entrepreneur is usually a solo or small firm practitioner. In earlier times, entrepreneurial practice was the norm. Virtually all practitioners were private practitioners rather than large firm partners and associates. The decline (in urban areas) of the individual, general practitioner who makes a living through service to a large number and wide variety of clients, and the growing ascendance of the large firm practice "are probably the most significant changes in the nature of law practice in this century" (Heinz and Laumann, 1982:16). The urbanization of population and corporatization of the economy have reshaped law practice, particularly in cities.

But while entrepreneurial law practice has moved to the periphery in urban settings it has remained at the core in rural settings. Entrepreneurial practice clientele are typically small businesses and persons of modest means. The latter are often one-shot clients who come for a marital dissolution, a will, or a real estate transaction and have no continuing business for the attorney.

Entrepreneurial careers have a built-in vulnerability. The practitioner must proceed under a double imperative—building a practice while needing to earn a living. Survival is predicated on ingenuity and enterprise. Creating a niche for oneself in a market already served by other practitioners requires deliberate strategy and strong initiative. The vital relationships are less with professional colleagues—as in institutional practice—and more with clients and people who can send you clients. Attorneys on their own measure success somewhat differently than their large firm colleagues. Success has little to do with professional hierarchy and more to do with economics. It is not a matter of making partner, but of making money. Career advancement for the private practitioner is as much a product of entrepreneurial enterprise as it is legal expertise.

Entrepreneurial practitioners—particularly in the city—rarely have prestigious and powerful clients, nor do they have extensive contact with prestigious colleagues. But they do claim a prized possession: autonomy. Their clients are theirs alone. Their time is theirs. Their decisions are their own. Whatever the economic precariousness of the entrepreneurial career, it is a career with a certain independence. This independence is perceived by the entrepreneurial practitioner as being central to professional integrity.

A half-century ago the restructuring effects of urbanization on law practice were sufficiently clear to polarize opinion about the meaning of the change. On the one hand, there were those who saw entrepreneurial law as the enduring standard by which all forms of practice were to be judged. E. E. Cheatham extolled the virtues of the Main Street lawyer as "a distinct species in our land. As an individual member of the profession he glories in his independence and his individuality; he is the principal guardian of the traditions of the profession and of the best that there is in our civic and social life" (Cheatham, 1938:13). About the same time Karl Llewellyn pictured entrepreneurial law practice as obsolete and doomed. "Antiquated in organization, in methods of doing business, in methods of getting business, in nose for where services are needed, the bar," observed Llewellyn, "finds its buggy crowded to the wall" (1938:133).

As a matter of fact, entrepreneurial law practice survives to this day. It is the norm in the country and—increasingly so—the exception in urban centers. Those facts establish the basis for differences to be observed within the entrepreneurial form of practice.

ENTREPRENEURIAL BACKGROUNDS

Entrepreneurs in the country reflect the social milieu of their setting just as urban entrepreneurs mirror theirs. The rural countryside is essentially homogeneous, and the backgrounds of the rural bar are very similar. Sixty-six percent of the rural sample in our study were born and raised in the county they were currently practicing in or in an adjacent county. Only 16 percent had come from a distant region. All were white; the majority were Protestant; and all were at least third-generation Americans, with Anglo-Saxon backgrounds. Thirty-two percent came from families where the fathers were in professional occupations.

Their single point of commonality with the Chicago entrepreneurial bar is that they also have predominantly local backgrounds (Heinz and Laumann, 1982:449). Local background in Chicago implies the likelihood of ethnic origins. Lortie's early study (1958:185) discovered that more than 50 percent of the entrepreneurial bar had fathers who were born in Europe. Carlin's later study (1962:24) of solo practitioners in Chicago indicated that more than half were of Eastern European background. Nearly three-fourths were born abroad or had at least one parent who was born abroad. Heinz and Laumann's more recent study (1982:448) indicated that only 12 percent of the personal plight practitioners considered themselves "only American." The remainder selected ethnic or nationality labels as identifiers.

Urban entrepreneurial lawyers have consistently come from the lowest socioeconomic backgrounds of the entire metropolitan bar (Lortie, 1958:212; Carlin, 1962:25; Heinz and Laumann, 1982:449). Their religious backgrounds have reflected their ethnic origins, with well over half identifying themselves as either Catholic or Jewish (Carlin, 1962:24; Heinz and Laumann, 1982:448).

The picture that emerges here finds the urban bar absorbing immigrant groups into professional practice but concentrating them in a style of practice that, in urban areas, has been moving from core to periphery. As corporate practice in large firms becomes the core, entrepreneurial practice—which is less suited to corporate representation—becomes relegated to a peripheral and thus lower status. Practitioners with lower status backgrounds are increasingly escorted into that practice. At one time German and Irish immigrants constituted the Chicago entrepreneurial bar. The process of ethnic succession has more recently moved Eastern European—largely Jewish—practitioners into that role (Carlin, 1962:21). The whole drama of ethnic succession in the larger urban context becomes mirrored in the composition of the bar.

The rural bar, by contrast, begins in a more homogeneous environment. It too draws its practitioners from the local citizenry, but there is far less differentiation in background among small town folk. Then also, there are not the vast economic forces creating core and periphery in practice as there are in larger settings. Thus homogeneous backgrounds tend to combine with more or less homogeneous clientele to produce a radically different entrepreneurial bar in the country.

An additional background factor that pushes the urban ethnic practitioner into entrepreneurial practice is law school training. Carlin cites the emergence of night law school training as having facilitated the growth of the ethnic bar in large cities. It was easier for the sons of new immigrants to gain admission to night law school, where the only requirement is the tuition fee, than to find a preceptor in a law office that more than likely was controlled by old Americans or more established immigrant groups such as the Germans and the Irish (Carlin, 1962:21). Two-thirds of the Chicago entrepreneurial bar in the early 1960s were graduates of part-time programs in proprietary law schools or Catholic schools (Carlin, 1962:25). The situation had not greatly changed 20 years later (Heinz and Laumann, 1982:445). For years, the full-time "national" law schools in the Chicago area (the University of Chicago, Northwestern University, and the University of Illinois) have been the primary source for lawyers going into large firm practice with its more powerful and prestigious clientele. The formula for entry into prestigious firm practice has been high birth, high performance as a full-time (day) student in a national law school, and the active assistance (sponsorship) of older members of the profession (Lortie, 1958:167).

The large urban setting with its sizeable immigrant population seeking upward mobility in an open society, in combination with the democratization of the profession, created the ideal conditions for the emergence of a "residual bar." Proprietary law schools serving this clientele added to the factors that have created a bifurcated profession. The institutional bar has drawn primarily from a particular national and religious background and a particular set of law schools. The entrepreneurial bar in the city comes from less honored backgrounds and less prestigious law schools and has been bequeathed the residual areas of practice not central to corporate law.

The rural bar rarely has the choice to attend a local proprietary or night law school. A full 70 percent of the rural sample took their law training at the University of Missouri in Columbia. Another 9 percent were trained at the University of Missouri in Kansas City. Only 6 percent attended law schools equivalent to the local law schools cited by studies of the Chicago bar. The centrifugal forces indigenous to the urban setting simply have not been present in the rural setting. Rural entrepreneurs are not only part of a relatively homogeneous rural population; they are also virtually indistinguishable from each other in terms of law school experience. Their law school backgrounds stand in stark contrast to their entrepreneurial colleagues in metropolitan settings. Their level of achievement in law school is an additional point of difference. The 1958 Chicago study reported that only one in four of the entrepreneurial practitioners ranked in the upper 25 percent of their graduating class (Lorti, 1958:212). Thirty-seven percent of the rural sample reported graduating in the top 25 percent of their class.

Finally, many within the entrepreneurial segment of the metropolitan bar had previous employment backgrounds and started their practices on a part-time basis while they continued selling insurance—say—or working as claims adjustors (Lortie, 1958:212). The vast majority (73 percent) of rural entrepreneurs, by contrast, entered law practice as their first and only job. Of the 27 percent who moved into law from a previous occupation, school teaching was cited most frequently as the previous career, followed by insurance sales and accounting. The differing routes to law practice among the entrepreneurial segment of the bar again mirror important background differences.

CAREER OPTIONS FOR ENTREPRENEURS

Yet another set of dynamics differentiates urban entrepreneurs from their rural counterparts. In urban settings there are career options. Those options are hierarchically ranked, with large firm careers at the top and private practice careers toward the bottom. There are a variety of other options, as well—including government careers, teaching, and in-house counsel opportunities. But in the rural setting, the entrepreneurial career is virtually the *only* career available. More than 87 percent of rural practitioners either practice alone or in two-to-three person firms, many of which are essentially office-sharing arrangements. Government jobs such as prosecuting attorney are part-time arrangements taken on to supplement private practice. Few businesses can afford full-time attorneys in the country. Teaching is, at best, part-time in a local community college or university.

Entrepreneurial careers are residual careers in urban areas largely because of the dynamics of the market for professional services (Lortie, 1959:359). In urban settings the professional market selects some individuals for core positions (institutional practice) and leaves the residue to the devices of enterprise. Law school graduates enter the professional market trained in law, and flexible. Some are able to land jobs with established firms, at which point they get their more specific socialization into the core law practiced in large firms.

In the large markets the number of lawyers seeking employment exceeds the supply of core positions available. Thus, some never get an offer from a law firm (Lortie, 1958:112). Those who do not obtain large firm positions appear to form career expectations more consistent with their immediate prospects. They become entrepreneurial practitioners. This sorting and sifting in metropolitan settings is facilitated by the flexibility that is indigenous to law school training. Thus, career differences

> are not defined as serious inequities. Longings which the system of work cannot fulfill do not develop; flexible men are free to follow the market. (Lortie, 1959:369)

Lortie drew the conclusion that in metropolitan settings

> men undertaking entrepreneurial careers uphold their course with zest and vigor—a subtle alchemy prevails whereby these men assume the values appropriate to their fate. (Lortie, 1959:368)

Carlin's findings (1962), however, do not support such a "subtle alchemy" occurring. He found deep dissatisfaction and demoralization among the entrepreneurial bar in Chicago.

In any event, an entrepreneurial career in an urban setting is an alternative career—and, in many instances, a career by default. In the rural setting, the entrepreneurial career is the only career—and thus is entered by design. As in the larger settings, entrepreneurial careers in the country exist because of the dynamics of professional opportunity. The difference is that entrepreneurial careers in the country are not residual careers. By virtue of the smaller scale market, they constitute the normative career—not the default career.

Our data suggest that the entrepreneurial career in the country is deliberately chosen rather than adaptively accommodated, as it appears to be in the larger settings. While the market's limited ability to create institutional careers in the big city drives many into the necessities of enterprise, in rural settings the attractions of home, friends, and local status as well as the highly prized entrepreneurial independence appear to lure locally produced lawyers into entrepreneurial careers. What is seen as a push in metropolitan settings appears to be a pull in the rural setting. Eighty-seven percent of the rural sample indicated they were practicing "precisely where and how they intended." While some of the same subtle alchemy discerned by Lortie may be reconciling expectations with opportunities among rural attorneys, the evidence does not detect it. In only three interviews out of 201 was there any suggestion that having an entrepreneurial career in a small town was a compromise of the lawyer's professional aspirations. One attorney said,

Well, I really didn't look for a job in a city firm. My law school grades weren't the best and my chances of getting a firm position probably weren't too good. So I looked around and decided to come here.

The vast majority of respondents, however, were represented by the attorney who said,

From the time I entered law school I planned to come back here and set up practice. . . . There's nothing in the city I want that I can't get by just making a visit there. Here I am my own man. Nobody's telling me what to do and that's what it means to be a lawyer.

BUSINESS-GETTING IN CITIES AND IN THE COUNTRY

The double imperative faced by entrepreneurial lawyers no matter where they practice is the need to earn a living while simultaneously building a practice. They do not enjoy the luxury of firm employees—who are handed clients, work, and a paycheck from day one. Business-getting strategies are consequently important to the survival of the private practice lawyer.

One difference between the urban and rural settings is certain. The metropolitan entrepreneur begins work in a setting where much of the business is already in the hands of large firms. He or she is competing for residual matters with other private practitioners. In rural areas, there is not enough lucrative work that can be creamed off and claimed by a single segment of the bar, leaving the residual to a lower stratum. In rural areas the beginning practitioner must start with what he can get, and often it is not much more than residual matters. But he entertains the prospect of building beyond that and, in time, having his share of the more remunerative business. Urban entrepreneurs rarely dream of rising above the residual category. They are not inclined to see a future where they fight their way into the core element of practice. So the visions differ even though the beginnings may be similar.

A second difference is also tied to the scale of the community. The metropolitan entrepreneur is often but a name on a door or a number in a phone book. Surrounded by the immensity of the urban enviroment, solo attorneys must aggressively pursue business since they are unlikely to be widely known. In the rural community, by contrast, the lawyer is definitely known. His reputation in matters legal, social, political, religious, and moral is the magnet that draws clients. In this sense he is like the elite firm lawyer in a big city. Clients come to him through contacts within an established community. For him it is sufficient to rely on reputation and the cultivation of relationships among potential clients. Thus, while the building of a practice in the rural setting is not guaranteed, it does not face the difficulty of anonymity.

While the rural attorney cultivates reputation, the metropolitan entrepreneur cultivates brokers. Because the solo attorney starting out downtown in the Chicago Loop moves in a world indifferent to his presence and largely unaware of his existence, his success depends in large part on his ability to create linkages with brokers—people who are in a position to refer clients (Lortie, 1958:250). These brokers may be other lawyers, accountants, real estate or insurance agents, building contractors, doctors, police officers, bail bonders, precinct captains, garage mechanics, ministers, undertakers, or plant personnel directors or supervisors (Carlin, 1962:135). The solicitation of relationships with persons who come in contact with people who may need legal services is vital to the establishment and survival of the urban entrepreneur. The relationship with these brokers is even more important than the relationship with clients. Most individual clients are "one shot": They need help with a single matter and rarely have a recurring need for legal service. Thus metropolitan entrepreneurs try to stabilize their practice by achieving a steady flow of clients from brokers.

The rural attorney relies some on brokered clients, as well. But it is not his primary strategy. In the intimate setting of a small town he has face-to-face relationships with potential clients. Brokers are less necessary. When a need for legal services arises, the individual already has a personal acquaintanceship with an attorney or at least possesses reputational information, which circulates widely in the community.

These two different modes of getting business carry consequences for clients. Metropolitan practitioners work in a relatively anonymous context. Therefore their relationships with clients tend to be superficial and impersonal. They rarely express anxiety over dissatisfied clients (Lortie, 1958:262). Their crucial relationship is with the brokers on whom they rely to send a steady stream of new business—from what seems to be a vast potential supply. The rural entrepreneur, on the other hand, is deeply conscious of the finite number of potential clients in the small community. He cannot afford to be indifferent to their dissatisfaction with his service. They have the capacity to talk and thus to poison the well from which he drinks.

The two settings for entrepreneurial practice thus face contrasting business-getting problems. Metropolitan practitioners suffer from the difficulties of anonymity. They have to struggle in the impersonal world of the city and rely on middlemen to sustain their practice. But they also reap the benefits of relative freedom from client scrutiny and unfavorable talk. Dissatisfied clients are less of a threat than disgruntled brokers. Rural entrepreneurs, on the other hand, escape the disadvantages of anonymity and the need to cultivate and compensate brokers. But they face the acute problem of accountability. Their work is scrutinized and talked about. And the context is small enough that the conversations matter.

In fairness to the metropolitan setting, those entrepreneurs who practice away from the anonymity of the Loop in ethnic neighborhoods are subject to many of the same constraints faced by the rural bar. While Loop practitioners have trouble attracting enough attention to build a reputation, ethnic lawyers in an urban ethnic neighborhood have less of this problem. Like rural attorneys, their task is to enhance and protect their good name "in what is almost a village atmosphere" (Lortie, 1958:266).

Because of the struggle with anonymity and the day-to-day competitive effort required to survive, the metropolitan entrepreneur is observed to have less concern with the broader responsibilities of lawyers toward society. The competitive struggle preoccupies the time and energy of the entrepreneurial bar (Lortie, 1958:212). Country lawyers are not necessarily more virtuous, less harried, or more idealistic. But they are more deeply tied to their communities and thus more likely to practice law in reference to the larger context. For one thing, rural attorneys are aware that the health of the community is the source of their own well-being. They are deeply aware of their linkages to the local economy, the local ethos, and the local politics. They have as vested an interest in building and maintaining a stable community as the urban entrepreneurs have a vested interest in maintaining their linkages with brokers. But the vision of the rural attorney is, by necessity, at a higher level than his urban entrepreneurial colleague. The country lawyer certainly strives to serve the specific interests of his client, but the larger interests of the community remain forever in view.

So the process of business-getting varies from one entrepreneurial setting to another. Because the metropolitan context is already heterogeneous, the allocation of professional opportunity is sharply conditioned by ethnicity. With core legal matters already in the possession of large firms, entrepreneurial lawyers compete intensely for residual matters. They appear to have two choices. They can return to the ethnic neighborhood where business-getting will be linked closely with reputation, as in rural practice. Or they can avoid the neighborhood setting and go downtown. There they must cope with anonymity. Their strategy will be dictated by the structures of opportunity. Linking up with brokers is both efficient and effective. Because of the intensity of the competition for residual matters, the metropolitan entrepreneur is suspicious of colleagues. In fact, colleagues are more likely seen as rivals. Because of the scale of the urban environment, entrepreneurs do not interact on a day-to-day basis as they do in small towns. Thus the necessity for collegiality is not present. Not that there is no rivalry and competition in smaller settings. There clearly is. But it is muted by the necessity to do business with each other on a continuing basis.

THE ALLOCATION OF ENTREPRENEURIAL EFFORT

The core difference between entrepreneurial practice in the city and in the country is that country practice serves the entire range of clients while city practice for entrepreneurs is essentially a residual practice. Heinz and Laumann (1982:40) discovered that well over 50 percent of all the effort expended by the Chicago bar was addressed to corporate concerns. Only 40 percent went to the

Table 4.1
Estimate of Rural Lawyers' Total Effort Expended in Various Fields of Law

Field of Law	Mean Percent	Cumulative Percent
Domestic Relations	15	15
Estate-Probate	13	28
Negligence (Plaintiff)	11	39
Residential Real Estate	7	46
Criminal Defense	6	52
Banking	6	58
Commercial Real Estate	5	63
Collections	4	67
Criminal Prosecution	4	71
Negligence (Defense)	4	75
Commercial and Contracts	3	78
General Corporate	3	81
Municipal	3	84
Agriculture	3	87
General Litigation	2	89
General Personal	2	91
Personal Taxes	2	93
Administrative Law	1	94
Corporate Taxes	0.3	94.3
Insurance	0.3	94.6
Civil Rights	0.3	94.9
Labor (Union & Management)	0.2	95.1
Public Utilities	0.1	95.2
Other	4.0	99.2*

*Less than 100% due to rounding
$N = 201$

problems of individuals and small businesses. As one would expect, the allocation of legal effort in the country is different (see Table 4.1).[1] Approximately 56 percent of the total legal effort in the rural setting goes to personal and small business matters. More than 50 percent of the total legal effort is invested in only five fields: domestic relations, estate, negligence (plaintiff), residential real estate, and criminal defense.

However, the country lawyer also has a variety (though not a high volume) of other matters as well. While his practice effort is typically concentrated in personal plight matters, he also does work for banks, smaller corporations, municipal governments, and insurance companies. His practice is essentially a reflection of the broad range of matters found in smaller towns.

Metropolitan entrepreneurs, by contrast, have more limited practices. Those who serve primarily personal clients have virtually no co-practice in business tax, general corporate matters, banking, commercial contracts, business real estate, public utilities, or municipal law (Heinz and Laumann, 1982:51). The circumstances of metropolitan practice limit the entrepreneur to a fraction of the total available practice. The rural entrepreneur—on the other hand—has access to virtually the full range of practice matters, but the context dictates that those matters will be overridingly from individual clients. The data in Table 4.2 illustrate the point by showing Chicago entrepreneurs to be much more likely to have no practice in a variety of areas where rural practitioners have some degree of co-practice.

Table 4.2
Proportion of Time Spent in a Practice Area, by Practice Setting

	% of Practitioners			
Area of Practice	Spend 30% or More of Their Time in the Practice Area		Spend No Time in the Practice Area	
	Rural	Chicago*	Rural	Chicago*
Real Estate	9	31	8	22
Business-Corporate	4	31	15	34
Personal Injury	23	21	10	36
Divorce	35	10	8	34
Will-Probate-Estate	29	9	4	15
Tax	1	7	44	51
Criminal Defense	14	3	32	70
Collections	4	1	13	54

*Carlin, 1962:118

THE CONDITIONS PRODUCING A MORAL DIVISION OF LABOR

It has been observed that "the system of which lawyers work in part reaches down into nether regions of the unrespectable and outward to the limbo of guile and force, which people may think is necessary but do not admire" (Hughes, 1958:71). It is true that, by definition, lawyers are often involved in disreputable matters. Clients have gotten themselves in trouble, and the arguments heard in court often sound like the "purified distillate of some human mess." Some quarrels are more respectable than others. And some types of work that lawyers have to do is more grubby than others. So it is not surprising that sociologists, observing the way legal work is distributed over the bar, have discerned what is tantamount to a "moral division of labor" (Hughes, 1958:71).

The metropolitan setting is where this moral division of labor becomes most visible. The volume of legal business is great enough to permit choice, and therefore those who can do so avoid matters that represent the seamy side of the law. These undesirable cases—the "dirty work" of professional practice—may involve matters that call for "influencing" and "fixing" and involve arrangements with clients and others that are felt to be professionally damaging. These areas include criminal matters, divorce, personal injury, municipal issues, and local tax matters (Carlin, 1962:18). Because these kinds of cases—at least in metropolitan settings—can be isolated and relegated to a peripheral segment of the bar, the process of differentiation within the profession is accelerated. In fact, the very demand for highly scrupulous and respectable lawyers depends on there being a residual category for practitioners who can attend nearly exclusively to the dirty work.

Carlin (1962:131) found that Chicago entrepreneurs were deeply conscious of their disparaged status and often tried to hide the fact that not only was much of their business with low-status personal plight matters, but that it was also heavily concentrated among relatively low-status ethnic clients. The immense pressure of the metropolitan setting to generate an exclusively ethno-religious residual practice was seen to be a source of profound frustration to that segment of the bar.

So the metropolitan bar is able to allocate its work out over its practitioners in ways that make it possible to practice exclusively among respectable clients with prestigious cases or among clients whose matters are stigmatized as dirty work. This residual area is relegated essentially to practitioners in the entrepreneurial hemisphere, on whom ethnic standing and law school experience have conspired to bestow inferior status even before they receive their first client.

The rural setting does not permit such a moral division of labor. Survival in country practice means serving the full range of clients and cases that small settings generate. The ability to differentiate between dirty work and respectable work may lie to some degree in the intrinsic character of the work being done. Defending sleazy felons is different from probating the will of a community notable. But the temptation to categorize work into morally contrasting types is mitigated in the country by the fact that nearly all the practitioners have some of each type of work. The norm in larger urban settings is to construct an essentially homogeneous practice—which enables the division of practitioners into discrete categories: us and them. In the rural setting the norm is a heterogeneous practice—which reduces the tendency to stigmatize cases, clients, and the attorneys who serve them.

CONTEXT AND PRACTICE SATISFACTION

An additional difference between metropolitan entrepreneurs and their country colleagues is in their levels of professional satisfaction. The Chicago entrepreneur—

> finding himself upon the lowest rungs of the status ladder of the profession, with little or no chance of rising, his practice restricted to the least remunerative and least desirable matters—to the dirty work of the profession and beset by competition from lawyers and laymen alike, the individual practitioner is frequently a dissatisfied, disappointed, resentful, angry man. (Carlin, 1962:168)

The rural bar, by contrast, is generally content. When asked to identify the practice situation in which they would most like to find themselves, 87 percent selected "my current situation." When asked how satisfied they were with the community in which they were practicing, 71 percent indicated an unqualified yes. Twenty-five percent responded with a qualified yes, while only 4 percent expressed general dissatisfaction. Overall, the rural bar appears to have deliberately chosen to practice in the country and they like the choice they have made. Very few indicated that they would trade places with colleagues in other settings.

Part of the anatomy of dissatisfaction among the metropolitan entrepreneurs comes from their dependent status (Carlin, 1962:190). Their ties to brokers, along with the ethically questionable tactics and arrangements for getting business and handling matters (including favors, gifts, and fee splitting), contributes to a general demoralization of the practitioner. The heavy use of manipulative skills in handling much of their case load—combined with the feeling of dependence on brokers—may often cause them to view the practice of law as more of a business than a profession. Many feel like parasites. Most feel that they are not respected by the lay public. They are at the bottom of a hierarchical order, and they know it.

By contrast, morale among rural lawyers was found to be consistently high. Seventy-one percent reported that their practices were growing more rapidly than they had anticipated. They felt intimately tied to their communities and enjoyed the rewards of status and social esteem that are available to special people in small settings. The rural bar also extolled what they saw as the virtues of professional independence. They prized their entrepreneurial status. They saw their broad general practice as the standard by which professional performance should be measured. While many of their attitudes are self-serving, there was no apparent dissatisfaction regarding their place in the professional system.

THE ULTIMATE DIFFERENCE: THE MEANING OF ENTREPRENEURIAL PRACTICE

It is a sociological truism that the meaning of a given social event or circumstance is not intrinsic to it, but rather bestowed on it by the audience or the participants. In this sense, reality is socially constructed and therefore relative to a given time and place. The ultimate difference between entrepreneurial law practice in large settings and the same type of practice in smaller settings is in its meaning. While their clients are quite similar and their cases are not greatly different, metropolitan entrepreneurial practice is perceived to be discrediting while country entrepreneurial practice is experienced as status enhancing. The difference is tied to the differing contexts in which the same type of practice occurs.

Most individual practitioners go into the practice of law out of a certain desire for professional status. But the metropolitan setting can frustrate that desire because the bar is so highly differentiated. The major players in metropolitan legal matters are corporations, large businesses, and powerful individuals. To serve the complex needs of these primary clients, institutional or firm practice was invented and now has become the norm. Entrepreneurial practice is a residual category, absorbing the matters that most institutional practitioners prefer to avoid. The cases are less remunerative; and the clients, less status enhancing. There is a virtually unbridgeable gulf between entrepreneurial practitioners in the urban setting and their more prestigious colleagues who occupy wood-paneled suites high up in the tower of a LaSalle Street skyscraper. Not only do the former view them with awe and resentment, but they also feel some disbelief that they are all actually part of the same profession. The institutional lawyers run a show that the entrepreneurs can, at best, only watch. The social distance between them is immense. As one Chicago entrepreneur expressed it, "Some of them in the big firms—they have such big offices. . . . I know some stenographers there" (Carlin, 1962:1976).

Entrepreneurs in the country, on the other hand, are the norm. The rural bar is essentially unstratified. Practitioners are essentially homogeneous not only in social background, but also in clientele. Most offices are clustered around the courthouse square or on Main Street. Some offices are more plush than others, but they are more alike than different. The clientele in their waiting rooms are strikingly similar, constituting a cross-section of the small town population. Entrepreneurial practice here is the standard and consequently is neither discrediting or deprofessionalizing. Private practitioners here are not marginal, their practices are not residual by local standards, and their foothold in the profession is secure.

In a sense, rural practice is "neighborhood" practice, also. But it is not neighborhood practice in the context of other types of practice. Thus the experience is different. Carlin catches this difference in the conversation of a Chicago lawyer.

> There was one thing I was concerned with—practicing in a neighborhood location. I found it irksome that people assumed that the good lawyers are downtown. They put the neighborhood lawyers in the same class with the real estate agent, insurance broker, and so on. . . . He's looked at more as a neighborhood businessman rather than as a professional. (Carlin, 1962:125)

A country lawyer expressed the rural perspective on entrepreneurial practice differently.

> Country practice is "people" practice. There's no way to have a purely business or corporate practice here. Over half of my clients are wage earners—what you'd call blue collar folk. But then over three-fourths of this town is blue collar, so there's nothing unusual about that. The five other attorneys in this town have practices pretty much like mine. They see more overalls than dress shirts too.

The entrepreneur in Chicago yearns to escape neighborhood practice and clients who are almost exclusively of ethnic backgrounds. He wants to escape it because there is more prestigious work downtown. It is the fact that there is a downtown with more prestigious clients that gives neighborhood practice its name and meaning. The rural bar has no alternative but to conduct an essentially neighborhood practice. But there is no derogatory association attached, because the context does not facilitate it. In fact, because the normative practice in rural

Table 4.3
What Is the Most Satisfying Work You Do?

	Percent of Rural Sample Indicating		
Type of Work	Most Satisfying	Satisfying	Least Satisfying
Solving Complex Business Problems	17	45	38
Working With High Stakes Cases	48	46	6
Trying a Case in Court	54	35	11
Helping Individuals	57	41	2
Helping Businesses	4	43	53

settings is "people practice," country lawyers generally evaluate it highly (see Table 4.3). It carries no stigma. "Good lawyers" in rural areas are defined by their reputation for helping people. That kind of work is seen as important, satisfying, and status enhancing. There is nothing else in the rural setting to compare it with.

So not only do entrepreneurial practitioners in the big city and in the small town practice in different geographical environments; they also practice out of decidedly different meaning contexts. Their practice type, their clients, and their cases may be quite similar. But they are worlds apart in their experience.

NOTE

1. As Heinz and Laumann (1982:ch. 5) point out, the attempt to measure the allocation of effort on the part of an entire bar is hazardous at best. We used the identical procedure to measure allocation of legal effort that Heinz and Laumann (1982:42) did, and thus our data are comparable as well as subject to the same risks and distortions. Every practitioner indicated the percentage of time that he allocated to the various fields of law (less than 5 percent, between 5 and 25 percent, between 25 and 50 percent, and more than 50 percent). We assigned 20 tokens to each practitioner—each token worth five percentage points of his working time during a year. If a lawyer reported that he worked less than 5 percent of his time in a particular field, we assigned no tokens. If he reported 5–25 percent, from one to four tokens were assigned. Five to nine tokens were assigned if he reported 25–50% of his time in a certain area. Ten to twenty tokens were assigned if he reported that more than 50 percent of his time was spent in a single practice area. Every practitioner had his 20 tokens (100 percent of his effort) allocated out over all the fields he identified as having work in. This may have required some arbitrary judgments regarding the actual number of tokens assigned to a particular area, but it did allow a reasonable approximation of how legal effort was distributed within a particular practice.

5

STATUS WITHIN THE BAR: THE RURAL STRUCTURE OF DEFERENCE

In earlier chapters we have argued that there is an ecology of law practice. The context in which the practice of law occurs is the prior and fundamental shaping influence. The subsequent differentiation of practice patterns, the emergence of professional stratification, and ultimately the very meaning of practice characteristics themselves have roots in the character of the setting in which a lawyer works.

Additional evidence of this structuring effect of context can be seen in how the distribution of honor or prestige varies by practice setting. The practice of law is a high-status profession. One can assume that those who enter the profession do so—in part, at least—to enjoy the prestige that accompanies elevated professional standing. Law has been demonstrated to be a source of upward social mobility for minority groups in metropolitan settings (Ladinsky, 1963; Carlin, 1962, 1966; Heinz and Laumann, 1982). It appears to operate similarly in country settings. At least 43 percent of the rural bar sample grew up in working-class homes. Their enjoyment of their enhanced status as lawyers was nearly universal in interviews. Frequent allusions to being "a big fish in a small pond" made it clear that the prestige of their professional status was understood and appreciated.

But the social standing of lawyers among those outside the profession is not our primary concern. Because law is divided into a variety of substantive areas (securities, taxes, antitrust, patents, divorce, criminal defense, corporate, commercial and contracts, and so forth) and because in larger settings these substantive areas tend to become specialized areas of practice, an internal structure of deference has developed within the profession (Heinz and Laumann, 1982:ch. 4). The lawyer planning to practice in a metropolitan setting is quickly confronted with an additional problem: How can I maximize my prestige *within* the bar? The impact of the large-scale environment has differentiated and so steeply stratified the profession that some practice areas are understood as discrediting and tarnishing to professional standing. In metropolitan settings the allocation of prestige to the various practice areas has created a highly visible "structure of deference" within the bar (Laumann and Heinz, 1977:155).

Our primary question—therefore—is, how does variation in context impact the evaluation of practice areas? Is there a universal profession-wide "structure of deference"? Do lawyers, regardless of their practice setting, see the prestige of practice areas similarly? Or is there also an "ecology of deference" within the bar? Do settings create unique perspectives from which substantive practice areas are evaluated? If securities practice is seen as the most prestigious area of practice among Chicago lawyers, what area of practice enjoys similar status among country lawyers? If the structures of deference vary from setting to setting, what is the logic of the differing evaluations? Before we address these questions, a further look at the concept of prestige may be helpful.

THE CONTENT OF PRESTIGE

Prestige has been defined as "a particular form of social power and advantage that is of a symbolic rather than of an economic or political character, and which gives rise to structured relationships of deference, acceptance and derogation" (Goldthorpe and Hope, 1972:19). Prestige judgments are seen to be subjective responses rooted in generally shared value orientations. They are presumed to be independent of wealth and power considerations. The possession of prestige certainly bestows advantage and power, but prestige presumably remains distinctive inasmuch as it is rooted in "the existence of some shared universe of meaning and value among the actors concerned" (Goldthorpe and Hope, 1972:25).

Other scholars see prestige more closely tied to the existing hierarchies of wealth and power (Shils, 1968:104). In fact, Shils argues that the prestige of social positions is determined by the degree of their association with the "core values" of the society. This suggests that, the closer a social position is to the reputed power centers of a social system, the higher its prestige.

The Goldthorpe and Hope perspective would lead us to presume that a shared universe of meaning and value might be discovered among lawyers practicing within a particular context. This shared vision would express itself in the differential evaluation of professional practice areas. Shils's perspective leads us to examine the relationship of these internal, subjective judgments to the more general core values of the society. More specifically, it prompts us to look at the relationship of the structure of deference in the bar to the reputed power centers in the larger social system.

This is precisely what Heinz and Laumann (1982:ch. 5) did in Chicago. They selected a subsample of the metropolitan bar and asked them, "On the following specialty list would you please indicate the general prestige of each specialty within the legal profession at large." A listing of 30 specialties was provided to the respondent, who then rated each specialty on a five-point scale—from "outstanding" to "poor." From these ratings a prestige score was calculated for each of the 30 practice areas (Heinz and Laumann, 1982:91).

THE CHICAGO FINDINGS

The orienting question behind measurement of the prestige attributed to practice areas has to do with understanding why lawyers in a highly differentiated system such as Chicago select the practice areas that they do. If we can correctly assume that the attempt to maximize status is part of the reason for choosing an area of law practice, then a variety of potential answers to the larger question come to mind (Heinz and Laumann, 1982:85–87). Certain lawyers may, for example, select a particular practice area simply to maximize earnings. Then again, they may wish to make money and also maximize their prestige within the bar. Or they may simply wish to maximize their prestige within the bar. If the latter motivation is present, two approaches to status enhancement exist. Lawyers can maximize their prestige within the bar by choosing practice areas that are most consistent with the *internal* norms and values of the profession. This would include those practice areas characterized by the need for intellectual skills and/or areas that reflect a commitment to public service. On the other hand, lawyers can also maximize their prestige within the bar by using *external* standards of evaluation. This would include the type of clients served and their relative power and status in the larger society. Or it might be the character of the cases chosen. In a system in which there is a moral division of labor and a clear distinction between dirty work and clean work, a prestigious practice may be predicated on standards external to the bar itself.

Consistent with the general findings of the Chicago study, Heinz and Laumann (1982:ch. 5) found a client-driven structure of deference. The most prestigious areas of practice were all big-business related: securities, tax, antitrust, patents, and banking. The areas judged as least prestigious were all in areas where individual clients are served: personal injury (plaintiff), consumer (debtor), condemnations, landlord-tenant, divorce, and general family. These fields of practice deal with personal plight matters. The most prestigious practice areas deal with powerful corporate clients. The data led Heinz and Laumann to this conclusion.

> Fields that serve corporate, wealthier, more establishment clients are accorded more deference within the profession than are those that serve individual, poorer clients. This suggests the thesis that prestige within the law is acquired by association, that it is

"reflected glory" derived from the power possessed by the lawyers' clients. (Heinz and Laumann, 1982:331)

THE ROLE OF CONTEXT

The Chicago findings are rooted in a particular context. The scale of the community is large enough to permit the growth of specialization. Within that metropolitan environment it is feasible to generate an exclusive practice, serving only one class of clientele. The bar itself is also diverse in ethno-religious background as well as in law school background. The combination of all these characteristics has produced a steeply stratified bar with a clearly discernable hierarchy of power and prestige. These factors facilitate the emergence of a structure of deference. In fact, the authors of the Chicago study, commenting on the disparaged personal plight area of practice, wonder

> whether these fields are disvalued because few practitioners devote exclusive attention to them or whether few lawyers specialize in them because of their disvalued standing in the profession. . . . The latter seems more plausible. (Heinz and Laumann, 1982:54)

The rural setting is a different situation. The scale of the community limits the probability of specialized practice. It is highly unlikely that a lawyer in a small town would have an exclusive class of clientele—unless it be a virtually exclusive, individual-client practice. The rural bar does not reflect radical ethnic-background differences either. It is essentially a homogeneous bar, even to the sources of law school training. The combination of these characteristics has produced a relatively unstratified bar. Hierarchy is most visible in income and virtually undiscernable along other dimensions. A high level of collegiality exists among members of the rural bar. Social distance is minimal. Given these significant differences in contextual characteristics, we would anticipate that, if there were a structure of deference in the rural bar, it would be substantively different from that found in the Chicago bar.

Karl Llewellyn grasped the significance of context for law practice in observing that

> Any man's interests, any man's outlook, are shaped in greatest part by what he does. His perspective is in terms of what he knows. His sympathies and ethical judgments are determined essentially by the things and the people he works on and for and with. (Llewellyn, 1933:177)

The rural lawyer is fundamentally a helper. Persons—not entities—are his primary clientele. Variety and volume characterize his daily work. Enterpreneurial practice is the norm, and its attendant economic definition of success is forever present in the thinking of the country lawyer.

Consequently we hypothesized that he would approach the task of ranking the prestige of practice areas very differently from his Chicago colleagues. First, we anticipated that the whole idea of assigning prestige rankings would sound dissonant to him. Working in a considerable variety of fields of law within an environment in which divisive and hierarchical differences are minimal anyway would seem to make prestige assignments contextually difficult, if not inappropriate.

Second, we anticipated that law school socialization would still have some influence on his judgment, and therefore his evaluations would have some affinity to evaluations of colleagues in metropolitan settings who had also learned in law school that some areas of practice are routine, unchallenging, and maybe even dirty work. But the extent to which these "memories of socialization" would override the pragmatics of current conditions was uncertain.

Third, because the rural bar does not have an existing professional hierarchy or clearly visible structure of stratification, there would be no framework immediately available from which to transfer evaluations. There is no residual bar, and no residual work, to guide the judgment. What would be available is a commonly shared value system about the desirability and integrity of entrepreneurial practice.

Fourth, entrepreneurial success is measured essentially in earnings. Therefore, we anticipated that, in contrast to the client-driven structure of deference found in the metropolitan bar, we would find an income-driven structure of deference in the rural bar. Practice areas that are highly remunerative in the rural environment would be judged more prestigious than practice areas that are less remunerative. While rural lawyers also valued the prestige associated with professional standing in their communities, they are not in a situation where there is a need to compete with colleagues to maximize professional standing. Whatever hierarchy does exist in country practice is associated primarily with income. Therefore, with prestige essentially distributed evenly among all practitioners in the rural bar by the sheer fact of their all being lawyers, the primary objective is profit. If status would be enhanced, this is less likely to occur through achieving an exclusive clientele than by achieving a high law-practice income.

Fifth and finally, we anticipated that practice areas uncommon in rural settings would not be evaluated as highly as those that are common to and characteristic of smaller places. Antitrust work rarely occurs in small towns, and therefore we anticipated that country lawyers would not accord very high prestige to such an area. The core values of the larger society may indeed focus on corporate enterprises, endeavors of massive scale, and power measured in national proportions. But in the rural setting, it is persons that predominate. They are the central and most numerous actors. Therefore, we would expect a tendency to elevate the status of personal client matters not only because they are so numerous in rural settings, but also because the values of the intimate community remain central.

THE STRUCTURE OF DEFERENCE IN THE RURAL BAR

A comparison of the field-prestige rankings made by the rural bar against rankings made by the Chicago bar does exhibit substantial differences (see Table

Table 5.1
Comparative Prestige Rankings of Fields of Law

	RANK ORDER			PRESTIGE SCORE		
Fields of Law	Rural	Springfield	Chicago	Rural	Springfield	Chicago
Estate-Probate	1	3	9	71	62	58
Banking	2	2	6	66	64	59
Negligence (Pl.)	3	11	25	65	56	38
Corporate Tax	4	1	2	61	66	67
General Corporate	5	4	8	60	61	59
Securities	6	5	1	57	57	68
Real Estate (Cmcl.)	7	12	14	57	56	51
Commercial, Contracts	8	9	15	56	56	49
Negligence (Def.)	9	10	18	56	56	48
Personal Taxes	10	13	*	55	56	*
Patents	11	14	4	52	55	61
Antitrust (Pl.)	12	8	5	52	56	60
Antitrust (Def.)	13	7	3	51	57	65
Agriculture	14	20	*	50	45	*
Real Estate (Resid.)	15	22	*	49	44	*
Labor (Mgt.)	16	6	13	47	57	53
Admiralty	17	23	11	47	44	55
Insurance	18	15	*	46	52	*
Administrative Law	19	19	*	46	47	*
Municipal	20	21	10	45	44	56
Criminal Defense	21	26	23	45	35	41
Domestic	22	27	29	44	35	35
Utilities	23	16	7	44	50	59
Environmental	24	24	17	41	42	49
General Personal	25	17	22	40	48	42
Labor (Unions)	26	18	16	39	47	49
Civil Liberties	27	25	20	34	38	46
Collections	28	28	*	21	24	*
Civil Litigation	*	*	12	*	*	54
Environmental (Pl.)	*	*	19	*	*	47
Criminal Pros.	*	*	21	*	*	44
General Family (paying)	*	*	22	*	*	42
Consumer (creditor)	*	*	24	*	*	40
Consumer (debtor)	*	*	26	*	*	38
Condemnations	*	*	27	*	*	37
Landlord-Tenant	*	*	28	*	*	37
General Family (poverty)	*	*	30	*	*	34
				Total Sample		50

Source: Chicago data are from Heinz and Laumann, 1982. Reprinted with permission.
*No equivalent category

5.1). The most striking differences are at the extremes. Comparing the five highest ranked practice areas in both settings, it is clear that the Chicago bar's evaluations are client driven (see Table 5.2). The clients represented in securities, antitrust, tax, and patents are typically large businesses. The rural bar, on the other hand, has a mixture of client types in their top-ranked practice areas. Both estate-probate and negligence (plaintiff) work are areas addressing individual client problems. But banking, general corporate, and corporate tax are all business-client oriented. Clearly, the rural evaluations are not client driven.

A more likely explanation is that they reflect an income-driven structure of prestige. Estate work—ranked first in prestige by the rural bar—was described by many country lawyers as "the land of milk and honey." It is perceived as being highly remunerative and the kind of practice that rewards seniority in the profession. High-income lawyers in the country tend to have extensive practices in this area. Twenty-eight percent of all those earning $60,000 (1981 dollars)

Table 5.2
Comparison of High-prestige and Low-prestige Fields of Practice In Three Contexts

Highest Ranking Fields of Practice

Rural Sample Rank	Practice Area	Prestige Score	Springfield Sample Rank	Practice Area	Prestige Score	Chicago Sample Rank	Practice Area	Prestige Score
1	Estate-Probate	71	1	Corporate Tax	66	1	Securities	68
2	Banking	66	2	Banking	64	2	Corporate Tax	67
3	Negligence (Pl.)	65	3	Estate-Probate	62	3	Antitrust (Def)	65
4	Corporate Tax	61	4	General Corporate	61	4	Patents	61
5	General Corporate	60	5	Securities	57	5	Antitrust (Pl.)	60
Lowest Ranking Fields of Practice								
23	Utilities	44	23	Admiralty	44	25	Personal Injury (Pl.)	38
24	Environmental	41	24	Environmental	42	26	Consumer (Debtor)	38
25	General Personal	40	25	Civil Rights	38	27	Condemnations	37
26	Labor (Unions)	39	26	Criminal Defense	35	28	Landlord-Tenant	37
27	Civil Liberties	34	27	Domestic	35	29	Divorce	35
28	Collections	21	28	Collections	24	30	General Family (Poverty)	34

Source: Chicago data are from Heinz and Laumann, 1982. Reprinted with permission.

or more a year spent at least 25 percent of their time in the area. The only practice area to exceed that percentage among high-income attorneys was negligence (plaintiff) practice. Negligence ranked third in prestige among rural attorneys (versus 25th in Chicago), and 34 percent of those who had incomes over $60,000 practiced heavily (25 percent or more of their time) in the area.

The top five prestige rankings made by the rural bar include three areas where clients are entities rather than persons. But each of these areas share the same characteristic as both the estate and negligence practices: They are highly remunerative. Banking, for example, is an area where the vast majority (79 percent) of the rural bar do at least some work. But only 7 percent do as much as 25 percent of their work in that area. However, more than 12 percent of the high-income lawyers spend 25 percent of their time involved in banking law. Their overrepresentation in that practice area suggests its financially lucrative character.

A similar picture is found in general corporate practice. Eighty-four percent of the rural bar report doing some work in the general corporate area. Many of these businesses are closely held (family) corporations and are not to be compared with the massive enterprises represented on LaSalle Street. Still, in the country setting, they are highly remunerative clients. While 4.5 percent of the rural bar have as much as 25 percent of their work in the general corporate area, nearly 9 percent of the high-income lawyers have substantial practice (25 percent or more) in the area. No one in the rural bar spends 25 percent of his time in the corporate tax area (ranked fourth in prestige). But of that 6.5 percent who spend more than 5 percent of their time in the area, high-income lawyers are vastly overrepresented.

The evidence for an income-driven structure of deference in the rural setting becomes even clearer when the lowest ranked areas are examined (see Table 5.2). Again, unlike the Chicago bar where the lowest ranked practice areas were associated with a particular client type (individuals), the rural bar ranks a mixture of client type areas as having low prestige. Only two of the bottom six are practice areas where individuals rather than entities are the typical clients: general personal, and civil liberties. All the others—public utilities, environmental, labor (unions), and collections—are typically associated with organizations or businesses. So there appears to be no clear client-driven logic in the rural data.

What does appear is a set of practice areas that are relatively unknown in rural practice and/or ones that are not known for producing high income. These variables are interrelated. We find that 88 percent of the rural bar have no practice in the public utilities area, and only 1 percent spend as much as 5 percent of their time in the area. Similarly, 85 percent have no practice in environmental law, and only 1 percent has as much as 5 percent of their practice there. Labor unions are not widely found in rural settings, so again we are not surprised that 93 percent of the rural bar have no practice in the area. None of these practice areas is associated with high income among country lawyers. Similarly, there is no extensive practice in the civil liberties area in rural settings. Two-thirds of the bar have no practice in the area, and only 4 percent have more than 5 percent of their work in civil liberties.

The two exceptions to the rule in the low-prestige category are general personal and collections. The general personal category may have been too abstract for most of the rural lawyers to evaluate for prestige, or even select as a category to which they could assign a proportion of their time. On the one hand, general personal is perhaps the best comprehensive description of a large proportion of rural practice. But after respondents had assigned certain percentages of their time to domestic practice, personal tax, residential real estate, estate practice, personal injury, and civil liberties, there was not a great deal left to assign to general personal. So it was apparently treated as a residual category. Seventeen percent said they had no practice in the area. More than half said they had less than 5 percent of their practice there. Only 3.5 percent said they had more than 25 percent of their practice in general personal. A disproportionately low number

(2 percent) of the high-income group indicated they had substantial (more than 25 percent) of their practice in the area.

The collections area was the lowest ranked of all the practice areas. This is not surprising, despite the fact that 87 percent of the rural bar have some work in the area. Collection practice has a deeply established reputation throughout the profession as being dirty work. In smaller settings it is often a source of consternation to lawyers because the defendant is almost guaranteed to be alienated as the result of collection action being taken against him. In small settings where the number of available clients is clearly finite, collections work is seen as highly undesirable (scored 21). None of the high-income lawyers had substantial (25 percent or more) of their practice in this area.

THE INTERMEDIATE-SIZE BAR AND ITS STRUCTURE OF DEFERENCE

We also asked lawyers in Springfield, Missouri, to evaluate practice areas. Springfield (population: 155,000) constitutes an intermediate case between the small-town and metropolitan contexts. Because the middle-size setting allows a degree of specialization in practice, we anticipated that the data on the prestige of practice areas would be somewhat closer to the Chicago rankings.

The full range of practice area evaluations in Table 5.1 show that Springfield attorneys do indeed tend to judge practice settings more like their Chicago colleagues. Four of the five highest ranked practices are areas where powerful and prestigious clients are likely to be found. The lowest ranked areas are all (with the exception of collections) practice areas where individual clients are represented.

The general picture emerging from the Springfield data suggests a client-driven structure of deference. There is the same kind of client-type consistency at both the top and the bottom of the rankings as is found in the Chicago data.

In sum, we find that there are differing evaluation systems, tied to the differing contexts. It is extremely difficult to differentiate law practice in small settings by client type, as is feasible in larger settings. Therefore it is not surprising that the Heinz and Laumann findings are not reproduced in the rural setting. It is also context-consistent to find the rural prestige hierarchy to be income driven. The primary measure of professional success among entrepreneurial practitioners is income. It is the mark of personal achievement. Within a bar that is difficult to differentiate in other ways, income becomes a salient consideration. The country lawyer who practices in areas that generate high income—regardless of client type—is cultivating a prestigious practice.

CORRELATES OF PRESTIGE

While it does appear that the rural bar is inclined to evaluate practice areas in terms of their financial lucrativeness, there is yet another possibility. Within the profession there is a general perception that some areas of the law are more deserving of respect than others. This is not because of clients or financial lucrativeness, but rather because law is a learned profession and those areas of the law that are more intellectually demanding are considered more deserving of respect. The intricacies of planning a securities issue or a corporate merger, for example, are seen as calling for much greater intellectual effort than handling a landlord-tenant dispute. Similarly, some areas of the law change more rapidly than others. This means the practitioner would be called on to keep abreast of new developments—which would add difficulty to his work and presumably entitle him to greater respect.

Law is also perceived to be a public service. Some areas of law reflect more of this "pro bono publico" content than others. When a practice area is entered out of altruistic or reformist motives rather than for profit, that may qualify it for higher respect. Work in civil rights cases, for example, is clearly less motivated by profit considerations than work in banking matters.

Heinz and Laumann (1982:101–9) identified five such "imputed characteristics" of fields of practice. In addition to the three outlined above, the five characteristics included an "ethical conduct" dimension, which hypothesized that certain fields of practice with a reputation for rectitude can enhance a practitioner's prestige, especially in a profession such as law that has a unique code of professional ethics. Finally, Heinz and Laumann identified a "freedom of action" dimension, which focused on the degree to which a field of practice enables the attorney to freely follow courses of action suggested by his or her own professional judgment as opposed to being influenced by knowledgeable clients or organizational superiors. This freedom of action dimension is associated with professional autonomy, which is reputed to be one of the characteristics distinguishing professions from other occupations. Thus, to the degree that a practice area is characterized as high in autonomy, it may be an area that deserves more respect by the profession.

Heinz and Laumann devised a method for scoring each of 30 practice areas along these five dimensions (1982:101–4). The resulting scores constitute a measure of prestige based on internal values of the profession. Such scores enable the researcher to identify the extent to which the profession's internal values are instrumental in shaping attorneys' judgments about the relative prestige of various fields of practice.

When the rural bar's evaluation of practice areas is compared with these correlate scores created by Heinz and Laumann's judges, it is yet more apparent that the primary criterion for evaluation of practice areas in the country is profitability (see Table 5.3). The three areas designated as highest in rural prestige are ranked below average (50) on the intellectual challenge scale. Corporate tax practice ranks at the top of the scale in intellectual challenge, and general corporate ranks just above the average. When the lowest rated practice areas are matched to their intellectual challenge score, four out of the five rank at or above

Table 5.3
Prestige Rankings and Imputed Characteristics of Fields of Law Practice

	Imputed Characteristics				
Rural Sample Top Rated Practice Areas	Intellectual Challenge Score (Highest = 67, Lowest =33, $\bar{x}$ = 50)	Rapidity of Change Score (Highest = 66, Lowest = 32, $\bar{x}$ = 50)	Public Service Score (Highest = 77, Lowest = 40, $\bar{x}$ = 50)	Ethical Conduct Score (Highest = 64, Lowest = 30, $\bar{x}$ = 50)	Freedom of Action Score (Highest = 70, Lowest = 35, $\bar{x}$ = 50
1. Estate-Probate	45	32	44	57	46
2. Banking	47	42	42	58	35
3. Negligence (Pl.)	33	42	43	38	46
4. Corporate Tax	67	66	43	55	46
5. General Corporate	51	48	44	59	41
Rural Sample Lowest Rated Practice Areas					
24. Environmental	61	65	72	58	66
25. General Personal	38	41	52	54	55
26. Labor (Unions)	53	53	51	47	42
27. Civil Liberties	61	65	77	64	70
28. Collections (Consumer-Creditor)	50	60	46	43	41
Springfield Sample Top Rated Practice Areas					
1. Corporate Taxation	67	66	43	55	46
2. Banking	47	42	42	58	35
3. Estate-Probate	45	32	44	57	46
4. General Corporate	51	48	44	59	41
5. Securities	63	62	44	57	39
Springfield Sample Lowest Rated Practice Areas					
24. General Personal	38	51	76	61	84
25. Civil Rights	61	65	77	64	70
26. Criminal Defense	51	57	57	33	64
27. Domestic	30	45	50	30	54
28. Collections (Consumer Credit)	50	60	46	43	41

Source: Imputed characteristics scores are from Heinz and Laumann, 1982. Reprinted with permission.

the average. The evidence would suggest that the rural bar attributes prestige to practice areas primarily on grounds other than intellectual challenge.

The rapidity of change scores reflect a similar pattern. If areas of practice that are undergoing significant change and require constant reading and updating of knowledge are—by that very reason—more highly respected in the city, then the rural bar does not appear to evaluate prestige by those same considerations. Rural attorneys gave the highest prestige rating to an area (estate-probate) that has the lowest (32) rapidity of change score of the entire list of practice areas. The content of the estate-practice area has remained relatively unchanged over the years. Again, the areas rated lowest in prestige by the rural attorneys are (with but one exception) rated near the top of the rapidity of change scale. So it does not appear that intellectual rigor of the work involved—whether measured by one scale or the other—is a significant consideration when the rural bar makes its prestige evaluations.

It is also of interest that the Springfield bar shows a somewhat closer kinship to the Chicago bar (see Table 5.3). Three of the five areas that the Springfield attorneys ranked high in prestige are above average on the intellectual challenge scale. We would expect this, since the practice opportunities are broader in the somewhat larger setting and the movement toward specialized practice is developing.

Despite the fact that small town practice is intuitively associated with public service because it is more heavily invested in individual client matters, the data in Table 5.3 do not support the notion that the basis for the rural bar's prestige evaluations lies in altruistic or reformist considerations. Not one of the top-rated areas achieved even an average public service score. In fact, the highest public service scores were identified with the rural bar's lowest rated practice areas. So, according to the Heinz and Laumann scale, one could not argue that public service considerations are behind the rural bar's evaluation of practice areas.

The ethical conduct dimension gives a somewhat different picture. Because four of the five practice areas in the rural bar's highly evaluated list also achieved high ethical conduct scores, we may be tempted to conclude that reputation for ethicality played a role in shaping the country lawyers' evaluations. But the picture is ambiguous, given the fact that the majority of the lowest rated areas also achieved high ethical conduct scores.

Finally, despite a strong endorsement of the freedom of action principle among the entrepreneurs who make up the rural bar, all of the areas scored as high in prestige by the country lawyers ranked below average on the freedom of action scale. The areas that they ranked low in prestige tended to be ones evaluated as being above average in freedom of action.

SUMMARY

The data we have examined suggest that the rural bar does not see the matter of deference as the metropolitan bar does. The metropolitan bar—operating in a highly stratified context—appears to judge the prestige of practice areas largely on the basis of the relative power and prestige of the clients who are typically served in the particular practice. Thus, practice areas whose work pertains to corporations or large businesss are accorded highest prestige. The practice area reflects the standing of its primary clientele. This logic of deference is feasible in the large setting where it is possible to specialize and serve an essentially exclusive clientele.

In the country the experience is different. The client mix is quite heterogeneous, mitigating the probability of a client-driven structure of deference. No one has a corner on the high-status clients to the exclusion of other types. Nor does it appear that intellectual challenge or any other reputed internal value of the bar guides the country lawyers' allocation of prestige to areas of practice. The most apparent basis for evaluation is economic promise. The structure of deference seems driven by profitability. Those practice areas that, in rural settings, hold out the best prospect for earnings are accorded high prestige.

This is entirely consistent with the character of country practice. The country lawyer is an entrepreneurial practitioner. He elected a practice type that emphasizes personal autonomy, personal initiative, and personal achievement. The measure of success is profit. The mark of standing is high income. This is not to say that high income is unimportant in other settings. It is only to suggest that, in a setting where the dimensions along which status and prestige can be measured are relatively constricted, the logic of using income is clear to all.

The data from the intermediate-size bar (Springfield) add further evidence to suggest that contextual factors shape the evaluative process. The Springfield bar stands between the rural and the Chicago bars on the deference issue. It would appear that, as the context gets larger and the opportunity for more specialized practice presents itself, a more client-driven structure of deference develops.

Because of the uniqueness of its setting—which means a uniqueness of experience and perspective—the rural bar takes on many of the characteristics of a professional subculture. Although it is clearly identifiable with the larger profession of law, its experience is sufficiently different to generate variations on several of the professions' themes—including the meaning of entrepreneurial practice and the allocation of prestige to substantive areas of practice. Further evidence of this subcultural tendency will be examined in the next chapter.

6

LAWYERS AND COMMUNITIES: THE IMPACT OF CONTEXT ON ROLE

The precise identification of the lawyer's role in the life of a community has both intrigued and eluded observers for a long time. As early as the beginning of this century John Dos Passos speculated that ''no one has raised the curtain upon the lawyer in his full relations to society'' (Dos Passos, 1907:5). More than a half-century later Geoffrey Hazard (1965) complained that research on the legal profession was still not telling us much about what lawyers actually do. And our interviews with practicing lawyers in small settings in Missouri in the early 1980s revealed that even they were surprised at what law practice involves. As one attorney expressed it,

> Law school is helpful with the generalities of practice, but the picture drawn in the classroom and the picture I now have after five years of being here are very different. I never pictured myself literally dividing up pots and pans in the back of a pickup truck outside the courthouse in order to get a marital dissolution settled. Nor did I ever imagine that I would be refereeing a dispute between rival factions in a church, one of whom wanted to fire the minister. Law practice is a cross-section of community life.

One dimension of the larger problem of describing the lawyer's role is the problem of understanding the complex interweaving of professional and community roles. It has been noted for some time that lawyers have an affinity for politics. Likewise, it has been observed that their rates of participation in community organizations greatly exceeds that of the average adult citizen. This raises the question of whether political activity is an intrinsic part of the lawyer role. It also poses the question of whether community activity is so closely tied to the core of lawyers' work that it is, in fact, an extension of the professional role.

For our purposes in this study, however, a more focused issue emerges. Does context play a part in determining the extent of extra-professional activities? Are lawyers in smaller settings more likely to be involved in political activities than those in more urban settings? If so, why? And is there a differential rate of involvement in community life between lawyers in differing settings?

PREVIOUS RESEARCH

More than 150 years ago Alexis de Tocqueville observed that lawyers are functionally important in democracies (1966:262–70). Since that time a plethora of studies have been done on lawyers in U.S. politics (Matthews, 1952; Schlesinger, 1957; Derge, 1959; Wells, 1964; Eulau and Sprague, 1964; Goldstein, 1964; Ruchelman, 1966; Cohen, 1966; Hourani, 1969; Bromall, 1968; Green et al., 1973; Hain and Pierson, 1975; Moon, 1977; Engstrom and O'Connor, 1980; Melone, 1980; Plumlee, 1981).

A variety of lines of argument emerge from these studies. Joseph Schlesinger (1957) said that lawyers are active in politics because of their monopoly on law enforcement offices. David Derge (1959) argued that the flexibility of law practice allows for interruption and thus conveniently fits in with public officeholding. Heinz Eulau and John Sprague (1964) identified an isomorphism between politics and law, which they called "convergence." This convergence would make law and politics a natural career combination. Michael Cohen (1966) argued that law work involves attorneys in the political process and makes them visible to politicians—thus enhancing the likelihood of their entering political life. Marshall Goldstein (1964) identified a particular sense of civic duty among law students that was leading certain of them into political activity. Irvin Bromall (1968) credited local factors in explaining much higher rates of political involvement among rural attorneys as compared with metropolitan practitioners.

The research thus far gives ample evidence that attorneys are overrepresented in formally defined politics. It also tends to suggest that political activity could be loosely defined as being part of the professional role of the lawyer. But progress in understanding the relationship between law practice and political participation awaits more detailed examination of smaller samples of data (Maru, 1986:71).

Less inquiry has occurred relative to the overall community role of lawyers and their participation in local organizations. Thomas Matthews studied the bar in Elmira, New York (population: 49,716), and found attorneys to be four times as active in community organizations as the general adult population (Matthews, 1952:81–83). He concluded that "community participation may be considered as one dimension of the professional role of the lawyer" (1952:162). The lawyer role was described as "complex," involving at least three dimensions: community participant, counsellor, and advocate. The permutations of these dimensions allow for at least seven distinct role orientations for the bar, but—Matthews concluded—"community participation is an expected, institutionalized aspect of the role of the lawyer" (1952:164).

In a study conducted for the American Bar Association in 1954, Arthur Wood and Walter Wardwell explored the relationship between the practitioner and the community. They discovered higher rates of organizational participation among lawyers than among adults in the general population (Wood and Wardwell, 1956). They also found community organization participation rates to be inversely related to community size, and concluded,

> The lawyer's citizenship role . . . is the penumbra of the professional role. . . . We may define it residually as those behavior expectations pertaining to the lawyer in relation to his community and society which are not those of every citizen and which are not part of the technical function of lawyer. (Wood and Wardwell 1956:162)

ENTREPRENEURIAL LAW PRACTICE AND COMMUNITY INVOLVEMENT

That law practice, politics, and community activity are deeply intertwined is clear. It is also clear that there are at least two motivations for lawyers to be involved in their communities both politically and organizationally. First, such involvement may be the simple discharge of what is perceived to be civic responsibility. Second, such involvement is a practical strategy for building clientele and supplementing income. How powerful and how relevant are either or both of these motivations could well be tied to the nature of the context in which practice occurs. As Bromall (1968:751) points out, one of the primary defects of most studies of lawyers in politics is the assumption that the legal profession is homogeneous, when in fact lawyers have significantly different backgrounds, significntly different statuses within the profession, and work in very different environments.

It is this latter point we wish to focus on, by asking how variation in context affects the rate of participation in politics and community organizations. We have already seen that the rural practitioner experiences a radically different set of influences in his practice of law than is experienced by the large-firm (or even the solo) practitioner in the metropolitan setting. Lawyers—like anyone else in any occupational setting—spend most of their time accommodating and adapting to the unique work conditions and institutional frameworks in which they find themselves. The norms and attitudes and styles of professional behavior take their concrete form not as one is preparing for a profession, but rather after one enters the practice and discovers what the unique environmental constraints of the setting are. The law student may learn a lot about law practice management and timekeeping; but until he opens his door on Main Street in rural America and finds out that the local citizens expect him not only to be accessible but also to provide free advice on a multitude of matters not directly legal in nature, he does not know what rules and principles he will follow in shaping his practice. Those rules come in the form of adaptations and accommodations to the realities of context.

The young law student who absorbs a vision of professional advancement that values starting as a firm associate with a specialty in tax law and moving up finally into a comfortable partnership role in a large, well-known, and respected firm will have a rude awakening when he views the landscape in a small town. He is then confronted with a decidedly different vision of professional achievement. The absence of the large respected law firm is counterbalanced by the presence of a small community whose respect and admiration he can win. The fact that there are only four other lawyers in town means that colleague recognition will be secondary to community recognition. The limited range of professional associations available in the county or circuit bar leads to an alternative involvement in local community elites. Activity in local politics, civic organizations, and charities all have a rich bounty of recognition and esteem to award to worthy participants. Public exposure along with personal and professional satisfaction are mediated by the community—not the profession—in small settings.

DIFFERENCES IN OPPORTUNITY STRUCTURES

We may describe the difference in contexts as entailing highly differentiated opportunity structures. In the large city there is an opportunity to avoid entrepreneurial practice. There is also the opportunity to develop a highly significant reference group among colleagues who are both plentiful and powerful. There is a professional community that meets regularly, bestows honors, grants recognition, and smooths the way to advancement. There is the opportunity for exclusive clientele, a distinguished address, and elite contacts. In this setting the pursuit of clients is often secondary to the pursuit of excellence in a technical specialization. The ladder of success is climbed by commending oneself to one's colleagues and peers first, and only subsequently to the community (which in large settings remains, for the most part, an abstraction). These opportunities open a particular set of doors for professional development, and outline a particular strategy of association.

A different opportunity structure exists in the country. It is entrepreneurial in character. The context calls for contacts and business-getting skills. Professional colleagues and the machinery of professional recognition are limited. Elite clients are rare. Advancement in a firm is not likely to be based on technical virtuosity. But there are other opportunities. One is not paralyzed by what is missing. Rather, one is activated by what is present. Therefore the pursuit of success will take a somewhat different form in the country than it does in the metropolitan setting.

The argument advanced here is that differential levels of involvement in politics and community organizations is—in part, at least—an adaptation to the opportunity structures present in a given setting. In general we would anticipate that as the density of professional interaction lessens there will be a growth in the degree of community and political involvement. This growth in community and political involvement is functional in at least two ways. In smaller communities where entrepreneurial practice is the norm, the building of a clientele is of paramount importance. Such clientele-building is facilitated by communication between the practitioner and the community. That communication is mediated most efficiently through local organizational and political activities. Therefore, in settings where entrepreneurial practice is the norm, high community involvement will also be the norm because it is functional for the development of clientele. It is also functional because it provides a generous source of recognition for practitioners whose own professional numbers do not enable equivalent recognition.

While it is true that the very structure and character of legal work is deeply woven into the fabric of the community and therefore we are not surprised that—in general—lawyers are more involved in their community's political, economic, and social life than the average adult, it is also true that the variations in degree and extent of involvement should vary systematically in relation to the size of the setting.

In identifying the positive functions of community participation for the development of law practice, one must especially recognize the issues important in entrepreneurial settings. Matthews (1952:116–23) mentions a number of ways in which community activity pays off for legal practice.

1. In a profession that has traditionally forbidden advertising, community involvement is a way of becoming known.
2. Lawyers are typically sought on the basis of reputation; and public involvement facilitates public evaluation and the building of a reputation.
3. As persons are met and acquaintances made, prospective clients are created.
4. Relationships with existing clients are reinforced by associating with them in social organizations.
5. Wide public knowledge is often an asset in handling certain types of cases.
6. Extensive involvement in the community helps to locate people who occupy strategic positions in the settling of cases (e.g., public officials, physicians, and so on).
7. Wide familiarity with the community introduces the lawyer to possible fields of practice.
8. The lawyer's interpersonal skills are often enhanced through wide social participation.
9. The lawyer's courtroom performance is enhanced by wide community understanding. It assists in selecting juries, decreases problems of establishing rapport with juries, and favors the credibility of case presentation.

10. Wide community participation also gives insight into opportunities for additional entrepreneurial activity and joint business ventures.

All of the foregoing positive functions of wide community involvement are especially relevant to entrepreneurial practice. The solo practitioner is perpetually in quest of clients. Most of his clients are of the one-shot variety, which means that cultivation of new connections is a career-long enterprise.

Our theoretical model suggests then that there is an ecology of extra-professional activity in the legal profession. In larger settings where the professional community is larger and the structure of law practice is more likely to be institutional, the role of the lawyer will tend to be more focused and technical. The level of communal and political activity will be less because the opportunity structure is different. The reward system will more likely be professional and collegial. The elective political offices will typically be full time and not conducive to interweaving with law practice. The pursuit of clients will be less an entrepreneurial enterprise and more an institutional (firm) endeavor. The lawyer role thus reaches less directly into the community.

On the other hand, in smaller settings where entrepreneurial practice is the norm, the role of the lawyer becomes more diffuse. The boundary between law practice and community involvement will be indistinct. While technical legal skills are still important, community visibility and assessment are also important to building clientele. Political office will often be part-time, enabling the maintenance of practice while also serving as prosecuting attorney, city attorney, or school board president. In entrepreneurial practice where the exigencies of building a practice are always present, there is a natural tendency toward deeper community involvement and nurturing the growth of a practice. That tendency is also seen by clients, who regard the lawyer as an accessible local expert able to do and fix a lot of things. It is in this context that the lawyer's citizenship role becomes the penumbra of the professional role.

ORGANIZATIONAL PARTICIPATION AND COMMUNITY CONTEXT

Our data allow at least a preliminary test of the propositions set forth above. While we have no available equivalent data on the organizational and community participation levels of metropolitan lawyers, we do have equivalent data from small rural settings and from one middle-size urban setting (Springfield, Missouri). Lawyers in these two settings responded to identical inquiries, and thus we can obtain some indication of what changes occur as context changes.

We asked attorneys to identify which and how many of 15 types of local organizations they belonged to. The organizations ranged from the chamber of commerce to religious organizations, and from service organizations to country clubs. We then summed the total number of organizational memberships and found that the rural attorneys typically belonged to more local organizations than

Table 6.1
Community Organization Participation, by Size of Setting

	Percent of Attorneys	
Number of Organizations	Rural Sample	Springfield Sample
none	2	3
1-3	16	26
4-6	27	36
7-9	34	22
10 or more	21	13
	100%	100%
Mean number of organizations	6.9	5.6

did the Springfield attorneys (see Table 6.1). Matthews's (1952:62) data from Elmira, New York (population: 49,716 in 1950), showed that the mean number of organizational membership in the bar there was 5.2. While Springfield is somewhat larger (population: 155,000) than Elmira, the organizational participation rate is similar. Dan Lortie (1958:212) found the participation rate among Chicago solo practitioners to be only 2.1. For our rural lawyers the modal number of organizational memberships was seven. For the Springfield sample the mode was four. The data thus suggest that there is an inverse relationship between community size and the level of organizational participation. If we can assume that the potential number of organizational affiliations increases as the size of the community increases, the inverse relationship discovered here strongly suggests a conscious and deliberate joining behavior on the part of the rural bar.

Five types of organizations appear to be the most popular among the rural bar. Sixty-eight percent belonged to churches, 67 percent belonged to political parties, 65 percent belonged to local business organizations such as the chamber of commerce, 63 percent belonged to service clubs, and 65 percent belonged to country clubs. Only two organizations approximated this level of popularity with the Springfield bar: Sixty-one percent belonged to churches, and 60 percent belonged to country clubs (see Table 6.2).

If one were to pursue the functional argument that joining behavior is practice-building behavior—especially in entrepreneurial settings—then the organizations selected would be quite rational choices. Churches are socially significant centers of activity in rural (and Springfield) Missouri. A majority of local families have connections with churches, and activity in them is frequently a source of positive evaluation by the community. Thirty percent of the rural lawyers indicated weekly attendance at church. Fifty-seven percent attended at least once a month. Church activity would appear to be instrumental in shaping one's image in the community and would provide extensive interpersonal contacts.

Political parties are also functional. They provide valuable contact with the governmental officials with whom attorneys must deal regularly. They are also the gateway to elective office, which opens legitimate advertising opportunities to an attorney—who is typically able to retain his practice while serving as prosecuting attorney or school board member.

Table 6.2
Types of Organizational Activity, by Size of Setting

Type of Organization	Percent of Attorneys Rural Sample	Springfield Sample
Hobby groups	38	39
Alumni	50	40
Business (Chamber of Commerce)	65*	36
Civic and Public Service	63*	33
Political Parties	67*	51*
Veterans	21	12
Country Clubs	62*	60*
Fraternal	40	29
Religious	68*	61*
Farm	15	7
Neighborhood	6	22
School	34	30
Youth (Scouts, etc.)	29	21
Charity or Welfare	41	47

*Organizations with more than 50 percent level of participation by the bar

Business and civic and service organizations as well as country clubs are more focused sources of community information, community business leaders, and professional elites. Community insights and opportunities are valuable by-products of these associations.

COMMITMENT TO LOCAL INSTITUTIONS

The impression given by the data cited thus far is that the rural lawyer is extensively involved in the community. Career and community appear to converge so that the "penumbra" phenomenon cited earlier is strongly suggested. This insight finds some corroboration in the responses of attorneys to the following question: How important would any of the following achievements be to you, in terms of your career? The attorneys evaluated a list of 11 achievements (see Table 6.3). Nearly 44 percent of the rural lawyers selected "a position of leadership in various community institutions" as being very important. Only 27 percent of the Springfield sample saw such an achievement as being very important to their career.

Additional evidence of the penetration of the local community into the professional role is seen in Table 6.4. Rural lawyers showed considerably more ambivalence when they responded to the question, Whose judgment should count most when overall professional performance is assessed? For the urban bar, colleagues were clearly the preferred reference group. Standing tall among peers is the hallmark of good work there. But in the setting where the size of the colleague group is small, the "structure of opportunity" changes. At least half of the rural bar in our study considered community and client endorsement to be an important indicator of professional success.

The question of whose judgment is most important when overall professional performance is assessed will create a debate in any context, but the distribution of opinion here suggests that the rural lawyer sees much of his activity as having

Table 6.3
How Important Would Any of the Following Achievements Be to You, in Terms of Your Career?

	% of Lawyers Ranking Achievement as "Very Important"	
Achievements	Rural Sample	Springfield Sample
Leadership in the ABA	0.5	1.3
Leadership in the Missouri Bar	11.0	11.7
Seniority in a Firm	54.2	59.7
Seniority in a Corporate Legal Dept.	7.5	6.5
A Strong Solo Practice	62.7	42.9
A Seat on the State or Federal Bench	20.4	16.9
Leadership in Local, State or Federal Criminal Justice Agencies	8.5	5.2
Leadership in Other Governmental Agencies	3.0	0.0
Leadership in Local, State or National Politics	13.9	7.8
A Position of Leadership in Various Community Institutions	43.8	27.3
A Position of Leadership in a Corporation	5.5	5.2

Table 6.4
Whose Judgment Should Count Most When Overall Professional Performance Is Assessed?

	Percent of Lawyers	
Groups Who Judge	Rural Sample	Springfield Sample
Bar Asso. Leaders	2	1
Colleagues	48	60
Clients and Community	50	39
	100	100

community implications—and therefore the community's opinion of his work should count for a lot. That perspective is less apparent in the large setting.

Not only are colleagues less likely to be seen as the final arbiters of professional performance among rural lawyers, they are also less likely to involve themselves in professional meetings. While nearly 80 percent of the rural sample indicated that the Missouri Bar was the most valuable professional association to them (when compared with American Bar Assoc., American Trial Lawyers' Assoc., Missouri Trial Lawyers' Assoc. and local bar associations), only 4 percent

Table 6.5
Professional Association Activity, by Size of Setting

Activities	Percent of Lawyers	
	Rural Sample	Springfield Sample
Attend Missouri Bar meetings regularly	4	22
Have worked on Missouri Bar Committees	27	66
Held office in Missouri Bar	7	8

reported themselves as attending Missouri Bar meetings regularly (Table 6.5). Springfield lawyers were much more likely to be regulars at state professional meetings (22 percent) and to have worked on Missouri Bar committees (66 percent).

The emerging picture finds the rural bar much more involved in local community organizations, and also much more inclined to see the community as being a reference point in the measurement of professional ability and to see leadership in local institutions as a very important career achievement. This suggests a systematic integration of professional and civic roles in smaller settings.

LAWYERS AS LOCAL EXPERTS

Small towns in the 1980s are not the soil in which a rich variety of professional practices thrive. Physicians are less likely to practice there than they did 25 years ago. Consulting psychologists and professional social workers are rare. Members of the clergy are often part-time or volunteer. Lawyers, on the other hand, appear to be hanging on. Their professional role has been shaped, to some degree, by the absence of other professionals. The vast range of issues they deal with, and the personal problems brought to them, all illustrate the community's perception of lawyers as possessing wide competence and a very general understanding of all affairs.

Evidence of this is seen in a number of ways. Rural lawyers reported an average of at least 10 percent of their time being spent on matters brought to them that were not directly related to the practice of law. For some lawyers, this percentage was estimated to be as high as 30 percent. Examples were legion. An elderly man asks a lawyer to help him get his name removed from a mailing list soliciting political contributions. The mother of a teenage boy reveals that she has found marijuana in her son's jacket and wants help in getting him to a drug counsellor. A widow asks a lawyer to keep her valuables in his lockbox. A jobless man comes in because he is lonely, discouraged, and needs to talk. Two teenage girls come into the law office and ask permission to use the copying machine to make copies of a pep song for the local high school. A father wants to talk with the lawyer about whether or not he should buy a car for his 17-year-old son. A husband and wife want to anguish over their decision to place an elderly parent in a nursing home. A businessman wants to know if there is room in the community for another dress shop.

It is not unusual for clients to go to a lawyer to obtain assurance and confidence. He often serves as a tranquilizer; he allays the doubts of perplexed people. Such encounters are not necessarily limited to the country, either. But we found not only that lawyers in the larger Springfield setting spend less time on matters not directly related to the practice of law. Also, only 10 percent of the Springfield sample identified such work as part of the lawyer's role. More than 50 percent of the rural lawyers felt that such extra-legal counselling was part of their professional role. Typical comments included, "If you can't have compassion and pity, you shouldn't hang your shingle out in the country." Another rural practitioner observed, "When I've helped to reassure a troubled person, it means as much to me as winning a lawsuit."

The opportunity structure in a small town drives many matters into law offices that in larger settings would go to pastors' studies, doctors' offices, chamber of commerce offices, or counselling centers. It is in part, at least, the absence of other alternatives that keeps the rural lawyer's practice so broad and shapes his image as a person possessing wide competence and a general understanding of human affairs. Thus his role becomes increasingly defined by the needs of the community. To be sure, some rural practitioners refuse to cooperate with clients who come in on non-paying matters. Some are "strictly business." Within our sample, there were lawyers who said they would soon go broke if they gave in to the pressure to be everyone's sounding board. But overall, there seemed to be an awareness that practicing in the country involves being asked to deal with an immense array of issues.

Alexander Carr-Sanders (1955) sees metropolitan conditions as transforming professions. Once regarded as "possessing broad culture, a wide special competence and a general understanding of affairs," professionals today in larger settings are seen primarily as "experts—persons with high competence in a restricted sphere. Great deference is paid to them while they act within their particular range but outside their role, they are thought to have no more claim to be heard than the man on the street" (Carr-Sanders, 1955:286). In rural settings, the image of a professional remains a person possessing broad competence into whose hands a significant measure of influence and leadership fall. That expectation helps to define the parameters of the lawyer's role.

THE FUNCTIONS AND DYSFUNCTIONS OF COMMUNITY ACTIVITY

It is clear that the small community is benefitted significantly by drawing the lawyer into its organizational and institutional life. His training in law has made him articulate. He possesses analytic skills valuable in solving problems. Handling legal cases gives him insight into community problems as well as community strengths. His adaptable work schedule makes him available for meetings.

But community activity—as we have suggested earlier—is also functional for the lawyer. It not only gives him access to meeting people, establishing a reputation, and attracting clientele; it also enables him to strengthen the community and advance its economic interests—which ultimately serves his interests. Our interviews with rural attorneys revealed their deep understanding and awareness of the economic and social health of their setting. They clearly understood the tie between the welfare of the community and their own professional welfare. There was little reluctance to head—say—the chamber of commerce committee working to bring into the community a Banquet Foods plant that would employ 160 people. Nor would there be any doubt about involving themselves in a program to develop a new sewage waste treatment plan that carries with it a generous infusion of federal dollars. The scale of the small community enables the lawyer to see clearly where his involvement will help to strengthen the town and ultimately his own practice.

But there is also a dysfunctional side to community participation in small settings. The necessity for partisan representation of clients' interests can, over the years, create a considerable group of enemies within the community. The two roles of community participant and zealous advocate for individual client interests are often in conflict. One lawyer who had been practicing in a small town for more than 30 years observed,

> As a trial lawyer I have made lots of enemies in this community. There are some things I can't do in the community now because of positions I have had to take in court. I've finally decided that I'll devote all of my time to my practice and not struggle with those conflicts anymore.

CORRELATES OF COMMUNITY PARTICIPATION

In analyzing the data on lawyer participation in community organizations we discovered that communities between 5,000 and 10,000 in population had the highest rates of lawyer participation. Smaller communities appear to have a less developed infrastructure of organizational activity, which may limit the number of organization memberships. We had no measure of activity in terms of hours per week and so forth, so we cannot conclude that fewer memberships necessarily means lower levels of activity.

While some studies have shown that family background contributes to the extent of involvement in community activity, the Missouri data do not reflect that. There was a significant relationship between style of practice and extent of involvement. Solo practitioners and individuals in two-to-three person firms were much more likely to be heavily involved in community organizations than

Table 6.6
Extent of Community and Political Participation, by Size of Setting

Activities	Rural	Springfield
Average number of community organizations in which lawyer participates	6.9	5.6
Percent of lawyers serving on "for profit" Boards	33	25
Percent of lawyers serving on "not-for-profit" boards	67	52
Percent who have been candidate for political office	65	18
Percent who have been elected to political office	57	9
Percent interested in political office	36	17
Percent aspiring to national office	1	8

persons in larger firms. This adds weight to the proposition that joining activity and entrepreneurial practice are functionally tied together.

In terms of practice areas, those lawyers who did 25 percent or more of their work in the personal injury area were significantly more likely to be heavily involved in community organizations.

The above quote about tension between community activity and legal representation to the contrary, the data show that in rural areas the level of organizational activity actually tends to increase the longer a lawyer is in practice.

POLITICAL ACTIVITY IN RURAL LAW PRACTICE

The data to this point suggest that lawyers in rural settings are more involved in community organizational activities than their counterparts in more urban settings. But the most dramatic contrast between the two settings is in level of political activity (see Table 6.6). Rural lawyers are three times as likely to have run for political office and more than six times as likely to have held elective office. On the other hand, Springfield lawyers are more likely to aspire to national office, although in neither sample was the proportion with such ambitions very high.

The vast difference in the rates of political participation appears to be tied, again, to entrepreneurial practice. The rural bar is overwhelmingly entrepreneurial while the Springfield bar is far less so. However, the solo practitioners in the Springfield sample were significantly more likely to be interested in running for political office than their firm practice colleagues.

Earlier research suggests that seeking and serving in political office is particularly functional for the entrepreneurial practitioner, no matter what the setting. Carlin's study of Chicago solo practitioners revealed that they saw political activity as a means of expanding the circle of contacts and as "a necessary expedient of building up one's practice" (Carlin, 1962:132). Hardly any of Carlin's entrepreneurial lawyers entered politics with the intent of making it a career. It was simply to bolster their legal practice.

The utility of political participation for entrepreneurial lawyers is not limited to business-getting. It also enhances their effectiveness in handling legal business, particularly in courts and government agencies (Carlin, 1962:133).

Wardwell and Wood (1956:306) found the incidence of political participation to be much higher among solo practitioners (56 percent) than among firm partners (40 percent) or associates (28 percent) in a large southern city. Career advancement was seen as the key issue. For entrepreneurial lawyers, career advancement means increasing the number of clients. For the firm lawyer, the criteria for judging success and career advancement are more related to technical expertise and competence. Political activity is less functional for advancing the career of the institutional practitioner.

The utility of political activity for advancing entrepreneurial careers has a long history. Lawrence Friedman (1985:560) recalls that, in earlier times in small communities, government was one of the biggest businesses; and therefore, politics was bread-and-butter work for lawyers. County, state, territorial, and federal jobs were sources of income as well as sources of advertisement for attorneys. The current data suggest that in this regard things have not changed much. For many small town practitioners, politics are still a recommended way for "scrambling up the greasy pole."

However, recent studies of the presumed symbiotic relationship between lawyers and politics suggest that the affinity is not universal. According to Bromall (1968), the defect in most earlier studies of lawyers and political activity was the assumption that the legal profession is homogeneous. His data suggest that political activity is a function of three things: (1) early exposure to law and politics through the family; (2) location of law practice (urban or rural); and (3) level of performance in law school.

The Missouri data confirm Bromall's finding in one respect: Rural practitioners are more likely to be office-seekers than urban practitioners. Part of the reason has to do with the favorable opportunity structure in rural settings. Many political offices are part-time in nature and thus fit well into a lawyer's life, especially if he is young and without an established clientele. The rural data indicate that 85 percent of the lawyers who had been in practice for more than 35 years were a candidate for political office at some time during their career (see Table 6.7). The Springfield data show that only 43 percent of such a group in the larger setting had ever been candidates. In more urban settings most political jobs are full time, confronting the lawyer with the dilemma of having to choose between political office and law practice. Furthermore, the ratio of lawyers to political

Table 6.7
Lawyer Political Activity, by Years in Practice and Community Setting

Years in Practice and Setting	Percent: Currently Interested In Political Office	Percent: Ever Been A Candidate For Office	Percent: Ever Been Elected to Office
0-5, rural (n=28)	67.9	39.3	39.3
0-5, Springfield (n=23)	34.8	4.3	4.3
6-15, rural (n=89)	44.9	62.9	53.9
6-15, Springfield (n=24)	20.8	4.2	4.2
16-35, rural (n=71)	18.3	74.6	63.4
16-35, Springfield (n=23)	0.0	39.1	8.7
Over 35, rural (n=13)	0.0	84.6	84.6
Over 35, Springfield (n=7)	0.0	42.9	42.9

jobs in urban settings is much higher than in rural settings. Political campaigns tend to be much costlier in urban settings, as well. Thus the functional benefits that political activity can contribute to the urban attorney are considerably less than those seen by the rural practitioner.

The Missouri data also support the contention that political interest is highest among beginning lawyers (see Table 6.7). More than two-thirds of the rural sample who had been in practice for five years or less identified themselves as being interested in public office. In contrast, only 18 percent of the rural bar who had been in practice for at least 16 years were still interested in running for office. The Springfield data also reflect this declining interest, but on a much smaller scale. We find that the attorney most likely to participate in politics is an entrepreneurial practitioner in his beginning years in a rural setting. For such an attorney the functional utility of political participation is perceived as very high. By contrast, as practice becomes more established, urban, and institutional, the perception of the utility of political participation declines.

The rural data offer no support for Bromall's finding that there is an inverse relationship between political participation and rank in law school. While the rural data indicate that 72 percent of those who graduated in the lowest quarter of their class were interested in political office as compared to 68 percent who ranked at the top of their class, the difference was not statistically significant. However, the rural data do support Bromall's finding that sole practitioners are more likely to be attracted to politics than firm lawyers.

Benjamin Hourani (1969) has argued that lawyers' interest in politics, political participation, and induction into political roles is closely tied to their struggle for improved work situations and mobility in the hierarchy of the profession. Consequently Hourani identifies two kinds of politics: the "politics of hierarchy" involve behind-the-scenes work on boards and commissions. His data suggest that the politics of hierarchy are typical of beginning lawyers while the politics of bargaining and influence are typical of stable career lawyers. The rural Missouri data tend to support that finding. The longer a rural lawyer had been practicing, the more likely was he to be serving on one or more nonprofit organization boards. While two-thirds of the entire rural sample were on such boards, this included 75 percent of the lawyers with more than 16 years of practice.

CONCLUSION

The data strongly suggest that there is an ecology of political and organizational participation within the legal profession. Lawyers in small settings are much more likely to be active in community organizations and much more likely to seek political office than their counterparts in larger settings.

While organizational and political activity are certainly functional for building a law business—especially where the practice is primarily entrepreneurial—the reasons for heavy community involvement in smaller settings are also related to the structure of opportunity. On the one hand, rural lawyers have the opportunity to serve in political office *and* continue their law practice. This is less true in urban areas. On the other hand, rural lawyers have less opportunity for colleague association and recognition. Their turning to the community for recognition and reward through organizational activity is a rational adaptation to the realities of professional life in small settings.

The whole process of adapting to both the opportunities and the limitations of the small community constructs a professional role that stands in contrast to the professional role mediated by the metropolitan setting. In the larger setting, the realities of institutional practice and extensive professional association focus the lawyer's role more narrowly toward technical-legal issues. The reference group is more likely to be colleagues rather than community. Therefore the role emphasizes colleague expectations rather than civic expectations.

The lawyer in the smaller setting, though, finds himself confronted with an expanded professional role. As an entrepreneur he must do what is necessary to get business. What is necessary is involvement. But he also learns that he is perceived by the community to be broadly competent and thus is presented with matters that frequently transcend purely legal and technical questions. His entrepreneurial mode of practice pushes him into the community. But his clients simultaneously pull him into the community by presenting him with a broad range of problems for which he appears to be the only local source of expertise. These pressures shape a professional practice role that bears the distinguishing marks of the context.

7

SOCIAL VALUES OF ATTORNEYS: A COMPARISON OF RURAL AND METROPOLITAN PRACTITIONERS

Our previous discussion has emphasized the role of community context in shaping the practice characteristics of lawyers. From their entrepreneurial mode of practice to their allocation of prestige among practice areas, country lawyers reflect adaptations to the smaller scale, more intimate community found in small towns. Even their greater involvement in community organizations and political activity are seen as adaptations to the opportunity structures unique to small-scale settings.

In metropolitan settings—where there exists great diversity in clientele and practice types—law practice has been described as primarily "client driven" (Heinz and Laumann, 1982). Lawyers typically represent only select segments of the community; and their roots are thrust deeply into the concerns, issues, and perspectives of a particular client group. The rural bar, by contrast, can be described as "community driven." Lacking a highly differentiated clientele, rural lawyers find themselves representing a cross-section of the community, rather than a segment of it. They are unlikely to have an exclusive clientele with which to identify terms of value orientation or issue focus. Their clients are a mixture of individuals and small businesses—a microcosm of the smaller town community. Therefore, their practices tend to take shape around the contours of the entire community, rather than an exclusive clientele.

To further test this emerging understanding, we gathered data on the value orientations of rural lawyers. The data were gathered with an instrument identical to the one used by Heinz and Laumann in their Chicago study, which enables us to compare the findings (Heinz and Laumann, 1982:ch. 5).

Three areas of value orientation were addresed. First, there were eight statements on economic values ranging from the role of the federal government in the economy to whether or not economic rewards are justly distributed. Five statements probed civil libertarian issues. Finally, three statements measured religious values.

VALUE ORIENTATIONS AND LAW PRACTICE

The impact of personal values on professional performance may be an issue in all professions, but it is of particular interest and concern in the legal profession. This interest derives from the direct relationship between what lawyers do as a profession and what their personal attitudes and values are. The lawyer is hired as a partisan advocate of a particular client interest that is value connected. This is most obvious in the civil rights issues. Representing a gay liberation group in seeking recognition as a legitimate student organization on a university campus is, by definition, an appropriate role of legal counsel. But it is also advocacy of a particular position on civil liberties, and thus entails personal values. An attorney representing a corporate client charged with violations of occupational safety rules by OSHA is arguing a value-based position about the role of government in the regulation of business. This, too, entails personal values.

Other professions have value-related issues in their practices also, but they tend to be more remote. The architect or the engineer does not directly address value disputes in the design of buildings or in the construction of bridges as do attorneys in the advocacy of partisan interests. Only rarely do other professions turn down clients because of social value issues. But such occasions are not infrequent in the legal profession.

Some legal issues are so explicitly value sensitive that organizations such as the ACLU have been established to handle them, rather than rely solely on the efforts of private practice attorneys. Similarly, the legal problems associated with poverty have given birth to organizations dedicated to advocacy of that particular set of interests. Partisan advocacy is inescapably value connected; and in many cases, quite visibly so. In fact, Daniel Pollitt argued in the 1960s that "the lawyer in the South (like his colleagues in other parts of the country) stands mute before the established values of the community" (1964a:81–86).

PROFESSIONS AND THEIR VALUES AS A THEORETICAL ISSUE

Of more crucial interest to the student of the professions is the theoretical problem posed by value consensus and dissensus within professions. William Goode (1957:194) has proposed that professions are in fact "communities within a community." He argues that the professional socialization process creates a unique set of values shared by all practitioners within a particular profession.

Practitioners constitute a sort of subculture, a "community within a community," and conduct their practice out of a shared value orientation.

Dietrich Rueschemeyer (1973:111–14), on the other hand, argues that the legal profession can hardly be characterized as a community in the sense that Goode proposes. It is stratified, fragmented, and operates within a pluralistic cultural milieu. He proposes that

> aside from those groups and social categories of which he [the lawyer] is a member, the most important reference group in private practice is constituted by his clientele. (Rueschemeyer, 1973:24, 25)

Thus Rueschemeyer proposes that a lawyer's social origins and clients' interests will combine in some fashion to shape the attorney's values. Because most lawyers work for business clients and the "sons of businessmen are the strongest background group in the American bar," Rueschemeyer theorizes that the bar will show a decidedly pro-business orientation.

Heinz and Laumann's study of Chicago attrorneys found neither Goode's community within a community nor Rueschemeyer's bar with a clear bent toward a business ethic.

> The overall picture of the profession's values that emerges from this analysis is one of substantial support for individualism and individual liberties as against concentrations of power in large corporations or in labor unions, and as against the authority of established social institutions, including the church and even the state. While the state's role in the preservation of traditional moral values is opposed by most lawyers, there is widespread support in the profession for the use of government power to redistribute social benefits and promote civil rights. But there is substantial disagreement within the profession on all of these issues. (Heinz and Laumann, 1982:148)

Heinz and Laumann's analysis of the structure of that "substantial disagreement" indicates that it is patterned by clientele differences. Attorneys who represented labor unions and the dispossessed show significantly higher scores on the economic liberalism scale as well as the civil libertarian scale they used. Such attorneys were joined by large corporate lawyers, who also scored high on the civil libertarian scale. On the low end of the civil libertarian scale were practitioners in probate and personal real estate and others in the personal business cluster. In economic attitudes, Heinz and Laumann found large corporate lawyers divided. Antitrust defense and securities lawyers were quite conservative while business tax and business real estate practitioners were more liberal. Practitioners in personal business and office practice fields were consistently more conservative both on economic and civil libertarian matters. The most consistently liberal on both scales were the lawyers in the personal plight field. Heinz and Laumann conclude by saying,

> We do not find that Chicago lawyers possess a distinct set of value positions. In this respect, then, the Chicago bar does not conform to Goode's characterization of the

professions as communities that embrace internally consistent values or have an identifiable, homogeneous culture. Rather, we find that, on several of the issues examined, the legal profession in Chicago is divided into two camps, roughly equal in size. . . . Lawyers' positions on economic and civil libertarian issues appear to be determined in substantial measure by the kinds of law they practice and by the kinds of clients they serve. (Heinz and Laumann, 1982:166)

The Heinz–Laumann test of the Goode and Rueschemeyer theoretical frameworks raises some interesting questions. Does the substantial disagreement found within the Chicago bar exist across other settings? Is one likely to find similar "structures of disagreement" in other metropolitan settings (Erlanger, 1980:882–903)? Do such structures of disagreement exist in smaller (rural) settings? Or does the bar in smaller settings conform more nearly to Goode's community within a community model? If smaller settings do tend to reflect more consensus, is that consensus attributable to professional socialization, or to similar clientele; or is it a function of contextual forces?

VALUE INFLUENCES IN THE RURAL BAR

A further test of the Goode and Rueschemeyer propositions about the legal profession's value orientation was done with selected segments of the Missouri bar. The instrument used was identical to the instrument used by Heinz and Laumann (1982:410–13)—which enables comparative analysis.

Our expectations were that the Chicago data would not be reduplicated in the rural setting. There were two reasons for this. This first reason was that the Chicago setting is a highly differentiated setting where client types tend to allocate themselves to particular practitioners, creating what Heinz and Laumann call two "hemispheres of practice." Such specialization in representation creates a highly diverse bar with considerable homogeneity of client types. That scenario is simply not possible in rural areas. Country lawyers have a heterogeneous clientele—a mixture of small businesses and individuals and perhaps some closely held corporations. They are hardly beholden to a single client type as is the case in metropolitan areas.

Because the rural bar has a very heterogeneous clientele—many of whom are one-shotters—it orients itself to the larger community, not to a narrow clientele segment.

Thus, the second reason for our expectations was that the general rural environment has the more salient influence on the rural practitioner's values, rather than some specific client group. This suggests that rural attorneys would reflect the more conservative values consistent with their small town settings. It also suggests that, while there would be variations in value orientation among rural attorneys, neither would they be so great as found among the Chicago bar nor would the differences be patterned by client types as in Chicago.

Value surveys among rural and urban populations consistently find more conservative sentiments among rural residents (Laumann, Marsden, and Galaskiewicz, 1977:598–600). Olaf Larson (1978:110, 111) reports that rural adults generally take the same pro or con position as do the national majority or plurality on questions of values and beliefs. In examining Gallup poll results over a decade, he rarely found the rural population to be in complete disagreement with the nation as a whole on any of the 136 national survey items examined. The differences were in degree rather than in kind.

In order to more adequately test our proposition that typical urban–rural differences in value orientations would be reflected in the values of attorneys, we also used data from our middle-size Missouri city (Springfield; population: 150,000). It was our expectation that the most conservative sentiments would be found among the rural bar, and the most liberal among the Chicago bar. The Springfield bar was anticipated to fall between the two extremes.

ECONOMIC VALUES

We can begin the analysis of lawyers' values by comparing the rural, urban (Springfield), and Chicago responses as a whole to individual value items as displayed in Table 7.1. Each column reports the percentage of respondents from each setting who indicated an extent of agreement or disagreement with the value-related statement.

Responses to item 1 (Table 7.1, Economic Values) show a significant contrast between rural and metropolitan professional orientations regarding the role of government in the economy. Less than half (46 percent) of the Chicago bar agreed with the statement, "The protection of consumer interests is best insured by a vigorous competition among sellers rather than by federal government intervention and regulation on behalf of consumers," while 44 percent disagreed. Rueschemeyer's expectation of a strong pro-business orientation is clearly not present among Chicago lawyers. In the rural Missouri case, opinion is far less divided. Nearly two-thirds agree with the pro-business statement while only 23 percent disagree. The urban (Springfield) lawyers in Missouri lie midway between the rural and Chicago bar, with 59 percent agreeing with the statement and 32 percent disagreeing. On this item, responses become more conservative as one moves away from the metropolitan setting toward smaller contexts.

In some respects, item 2 is not only an indicator of economic perspective; it is also a referendum on bigness. The bar in all settings are more inclined to agree than to disagree with this statement, with the rural sample somewhat more conservative than the Chicago bar. The more conservative the orientation, the greater the likelihood to disagree with the statement. But in rural areas, bigness is not perceived as a virtue—which may have muted a more powerfully conservative response.

In items 3 and 4 the contrast becomes much clearer again. Big unions are judged by nearly 75 percent of the rural bar not to be in the interest of the country while only 53 percent of the Chicago bar felt that way. Rural lawyers

Table 7.1
Comparison of Rural, Urban, and Metropolitan Lawyers' Attitudes on Selected Economic and Civil Liberties Issues

Value Statements		Percent of Lawyers					
		Strongly Agree (5)	Agree (4)	Undecided (3)	Disagree (2)	Strongly Disagree (1)	$\bar{X}$
Economic Values							
1. The protection of consumer interests is best insured by a vigorous competition among sellers rather than by federal government intervention and regulation on behalf of consumers.	Rural	30	35	11	20	3	3.70*
	Urban	23	36	9	29	3	3.49
	Chicago	17	29	11	33	11	3.11
2. There is too much power concentrated in the hands of a few large companies for the good of the country.	Rural	9	40	16	30	5	3.18
	Urban	14	33	25	26	3	3.30
	Chicago	16	36	17	26	5	3.33
3. Labor unions have become too big for the good of the country	Rural	30	42	10	17	1	3.83**
	Urban	17	52	13	12	7	3.61
	Chicago	21	32	21	22	4	3.49
4. The gains that labor unions make for their members help make the country more prosperous.	Rural	2	28	20	39	11	2.69
	Urban	4	23	20	43	10	2.68
	Chicago	3	36	26	28	8	3.01
5. Differences in income among occupations should be reduced	Rural	1	7	5	61	27	1.95**
	Urban	3	13	10	52	22	2.22
	Chicago	5	9	12	47	26	2.17
6. All Americans should have equal access to quality medical care regardless of ability to pay	Rural	9	54	19	16	2	3.52**
	Urban	13	60	16	9	3	3.71
	Chicago	41	46	7	6	1	4.23
7. One of the most important roles of government is to help those who cannot help themselves, such as the poor, the disadvantaged, and the unemployed	Rural	9	55	7	24	5	3.37
	Urban	12	48	9	29	3	3.38
	Chicago	26	52	7	13	3	3.88
8. Economic profits are by and large justly distributed in the U.S. today	Rural	3	39	17	36	5	2.98
	Urban	3	33	26	30	9	2.90
	Chicago	3	23	20	41	14	2.63

Value Statements		Percent of Lawyers					
		Strongly Agree (5)	Agree (4)	Undecided (3)	Disagree (2)	Strongly Disagree (1)	X
Civil Libertarian Values							
1. The right to associate with whom one pleases is being endangered by the excesses of civil rights legislation	Rural	8	19	16	47	10	2.69**
	Urban	5	16	9	56	14	2.42
	Chicago	7	18	12	41	22	2.47
2. Preservation of the traditional moral values of the community in such areas as prostitution, gambling, and homosexuality is a perfectly legitimate objective of the criminal law	Rural	10	51	11	23	5	3.38
	Urban	7	46	19	22	6	3.23
	Chicago	8	29	13	34	16	2.79
3. The provisions of the U.S. Constitution should be construed strictly so as to implement the intent of the framers	Rural	11	43	12	31	3	3.28
	Urban	10	38	12	38	2	3.16
	Chicago	8	27	10	44	12	2.78
4. A group of feminists remove all their clothing in public at the site of a Hugh Hefner speech in order to protest *Playboy*'s treatment of women as "sex objects." To punish them for indecent exposure would abridge their right to public expression	Rural	3	17	10	60	10	2.43**
	Urban	7	25	9	51	9	2.69
	Chicago	6	22	12	50	10	2.64
5. Publishing a directory of homosexuals, describing the acts that they are willing and available to perform, should be punishable as a conspiracy to corrupt public morals	Rural	8	26	15	40	10	2.82
	Urban	8	23	29	35	5	2.94
	Chicago	8	18	19	39	16	2.63

Table 7.1 (continued)

Value Statements		Percent of Lawyers					
		Strongly Agree (5)	Agree (4)	Undecided (3)	Disagree (2)	Strongly Disagree (1)	X
Religious Values							
1. To lead a good life it is necessary for a person to be guided by the teachings and beliefs of an established religious group	Rural	17	33	13	30	7	3.23**
	Urban	12	27	13	36	12	2.91
	Chicago	10	18	12	35	25	2.53
2. Churches are necessary to establish and preserve concepts of right and wrong.	Rural	14	54	14	15	3	3.60
	Urban	20	43	12	18	8	3.48
	Chicago	11	32	17	28	12	3.02
3. A man ought to be guided by what his experience tells him is right rather than by what any institution, such as church or government, tells him to do.	Rural	13	42	15	28	2	3.36
	Urban	20	33	18	29	0	3.43
	Chicago	21	40	15	20	5	3.55
Economic Liberalism Mean Score							
Rural	2.78						
Urban	2.93						
Chicago	3.23						
Civil Libertarian Mean Score							
Rural	2.72						
Urban	2.76						
Chicago	3.28						
Religious Values Mean Score							
Rural	3.14						
Urban	2.98						
Chicago	2.82						

Source: Chicago data are from Heinz and Laumann, 1982. Reprinted with permission.
*Difference between rural and urban means significant at < .10 level
**Significant at < .05 level

also disagreed with the notion that gains the labor unions had made for their members help make the country more prosperous, while Chicago lawyers were more inclined to agree than to disagree.

The first four items show the Chicago bar in rather general agreement that concentrations of power—whether in large business or large unions—are undesirable. The pro-business mentality predicted by Rueschemeyer is clearly absent. The rural bar, on the other hand, is somewhat more divided over the issue of concentrations of power. They are overwhelmingly opposed to concentration of power in labor unions, but less convinced that there is too much power concentrated in a few large companies. So the rural bar more nearly conforms to Rueschemeyer's expectations despite the fact that a relatively small percent of rural lawyers come from business family backgrounds and there are relatively fewer business clients in rural settings.

Items 5 through 8 measure attitudes toward a "welfare state mentality." As expected, few lawyers in any of the settings agreed that differences in income among occupations should be reduced (item 5). The conservative presumption is that one gets what one earns. But it is noteworthy that rural lawyers were most emphatic in their conservatism (88 percent disagreeing, compared with 73 percent of the Chicago sample). A similar outcome is noted in item 6. While the majority of lawyers from all settings agreed that all Americans should have equal access to quality medical care regardless of ability to pay, the rural majority was only 63 percent as compared to the Chicago bar showing 87 percent who agreed with the statement.

Again in item 7, the majority of all lawyers agreed that government has an important role in helping the helpless. But the rural bar showed only 64 percent agreement while the Chicago bar showed 78 percent agreement.

The final item (8) in the economic values section of the inquiry stated that economic profits are, by and large, justly distributed in the United States today. The more conservative the attitude, the more likely one is to agree with that statement. Forty-two percent of the rural bar agreed while only 26 percent of the Chicago bar agreed.

The responses to these four items further underscore what was implied in the earlier items. Chicago lawyers, serving a much higher proportion of business clients and reflecting a higher proportion of business family backgrounds, nonetheless do not show the strong pro-business orientation that Rueschemeyer predicted. In fact, they are strikingly supportive of what might be characterized as a "welfare state mentality." They see economic profits as maldistributed, government as having a primary role in assisting the needy, and citizen entitlement to medical care regardless of income. By contrast, the rural sample shows a more conservative orientation. While it did not take an opposite position to the Chicago bar on any of the items, it consistently took a more conservative position. It should be noted, however, that the Chicago data were gathered in the mid–1970s, shortly after the Nixon resignation. By contrast, the rural data were gathered during the Reagan years. Whether the differing political environments affected lawyers' attitudes is open to conjecture. It would seem unlikely, however, that the extent of difference between the Chicago data and the rural data could be adequately accounted for by the different time frames in which they were collected.

These data suggest that Goode's notion of a unique set of values emerging as a result of the socialization process in law school is unlikely. Rather than lawyers being a unique community within a community, the data suggest that lawyers tend to reflect their containing communities. In the cosmopolitan (Chicago) setting, lawyers' economic attitudes tend to be diverse but in a liberal direction, typical of urban populations as a whole. In rural settings, the bar tends to show a more conservative orientation, consistent with the general perspective of that setting. While we have no exactly comparable data in which rural and urban populations are measured along exactly the same dimensions used for this bar study, the evidence we do have suggests that lawyers tend to reflect their *settings* on economic issues rather than their professional socialization.

Moreover, the greater inclination toward a business mentality in the rural setting—where both the family backgrounds are less business related and the relative numbers of business clients are fewer than in metropolitan settings—tends to call into question Rueschemeyer's suggestion that a business mentality among lawyers is derived from clientele and family background influences.

What we may be seeing here, especially in the rural bar, is an inclination to reflect the conservatism implicit in rural settings. There may also be a unique confluence of factors that produces the more conservative business orientation in the country. Rural law practice is primarily entrepreneurial practice. Lawyers are typically small-business people, not firm employees. That fact combining with the traditional moral orientations and instrumental activism typical of rural settings may go further in explaining the rural data than Rueschemeyer's conjectures about the bar as a whole.

CIVIL LIBERTARIAN VALUES

While lawyers do spend a great deal of their time working with matters that relate to financial and property transactions and other issues dealing with economic justice, they also deal with matters related to individual and group rights and liberties. Consequently their attitudes toward civil libertarian issues are also of interest.

We used the identical set of five items used with the Chicago bar. Item 1 (Table 7.1, Civil Libertarian Values) proposes that "the right to associate with whom one pleases is being endangered by the excesses of civil rights legislation." The strong disgreement of lawyers in all settings with this statement is not surprising, given their relatively elite status in the social hierarchy, as well as their training in law—which includes the Bill of Rights. But again, the rural sample shows a significantly more conservative attitude toward the issue than either the Springfield or Chicago bar.

A more distinct difference is seen in item 2. Here it is proposed that the ''preservation of the traditional moral values of the community in such areas as prostitution, gambling, and homosexuality is a perfectly legitimate objective of the criminal law.'' Chicago lawyers, while divided on this issue, tended to disagree with the statement (50 percent disagreeing; 37 percent agreeing). Rural lawyers—on the other hand—showed a quite different orientation. Only 28 percent disagreed while 61 percent agreed with the proposition. Again, the Springfield sample took the middle ground, though still with a majority agreeing. The conservatism of the rural environment is most explicit in moral issues. Thus, it is not surprising that, on this proposition, rural attorneys are not only on the opposite end of the continuum from their metropolitan colleagues, but also on the opposite pole in sentiment.

A similar contrast in orientation is seen in item 3, which proposes that ''the provisions of the U.S. Constitution should be construed strictly so as to implement the intent of the framers.'' Only 35 percent of the Chicago bar agreed. Fifty-four percent of the rural bar agreed. The Springfield bar again lay midway between, with 48 percent in agreement and 40 percent in disagreement.

Items 4 and 5 represent more radical civil libertarian issues of free speech. Only 20 percent of rural lawyers felt that punishing feminists for removing their clothes in protest of a Hugh Hefner speech would abridge their right to public expression. Twenty-eight percent of Chicago lawyers agreed with that sentiment reflecting a more liberal attitude which is consistent with earlier findings. But on the question of whether publishing a directory of homosexuals, describing the acts that they are willing and available to perform, should be punishable as a conspiracy to corrupt public morals, rural lawyers turned out to be slightly more liberal than Chicago attorneys, a rather counter-intuitive finding.

The overall finding of the civil libertarian scale is that a significant difference does exist between Chicago lawyers and the rural and Springfield, Missouri, lawyers. The Chicago bar appears to be more client oriented than law or court oriented in civil libertarian matters. Despite the fact that Illinois law proscribes prostitution, gambling, and to a lesser extent homosexuality, Chicago lawyers were not inclined to endorse existing legislation above the perceived rights of individuals. The Chicago sample appears to value individual liberty or privacy in these matters above compliance with prescribed norms of moral conduct. In the two items (4 and 5) where (extreme) specific instances of freedom of speech are raised, rural lawyers tend to agree with Chicago lawyers—but in one case, more conservatively. In items 2 and 3, rural lawyers part company with their cosmopolitan counterparts and show a tendency to defend the law as opposed to defending presumed individual rights. In this sense the lawyer's role as an officer of the court appears to take precedence over his role as a partisan advocate in matters of civil liberties. This again is consistent with the overall tendency of rural conservatism to be most apparent on moral issues (Larson, 1978:96).

RELIGIOUS VALUES

Because there is an obvious connection between the extent of support for traditional moral values and the extent of support for religion and its institutions, the value survey also included three religious items (see Table 7.1, Religious Values).

Items 1 and 2 focus on the importance of institutional religion. Half of the rural lawyers agreed that to lead a good life it was necessary to be guided by the teachings of an established religious group. Only 28 percent of the Chicago sample agreed with that idea. Rural practitioners were also supportive (68 percent) of the idea that churches are necessary to preserve concepts of right and wrong, while Chicago lawyers were less certain of that (43 percent). Responses to both of these items reflect a more conservative religious orientation on the part of the rural bar.

However, the rural bar confounds logic by also affirming the idea that "a man ought to be guided by what his experience tells him is right rather than by what any institution, such as church or government, tells him to do." Fifty-five percent of the rural bar agree with that view whereas 61 percent of the Chicago bar agree with it. The Chicago bar's response was more consistent with their earlier skepticism about the role of institutional religion.

These data are not surprising, given the stronger hold on traditional values typical of rural environments. Also, given the inclination of Chicago lawyers not to support the authority of institutions—whether churches or government—it is not surprising that they were inclined to trust their own experience rather than what institutions tell them. The clear consensus of the rural bar on the religious questions reflects what other surveys have found consistently in rural areas—that "a larger proportion of rural people [than others] rate themselves as 'very' or 'fairly' religious" (Larson, 1978:100). As Larson asserts, "To a greater extent rural people believe that religion can answer 'all or most of today's problems' rather than being 'old fashioned and out of date.' "

THE RURAL INFLUENCE

The rural data when compared with the Chicago data on economic, civil libertarian, and religious issues show the following characteristics:

1. On individual items as well as on the scale mean scores, the rural bar is consistently more conservative in social values than the Chicago bar.
2. While there is evidence of value pluralism in all the data, a somewhat greater consensus exists among the rural bar on value matters than is to be found in the metropolitan bar. In those instances in which greater consensus exists among the Chicago bar it is in terms of a more powerful liberalism. Even though the rural bar is inclined to be liberal on many of the same issues, it is less decisively so.
3. There is a greater evidence of entrepreneurial values in the rural bar with its greater endorsement of the role of competition, its anti-union orientation, its support for income differences among occupations, and its stronger endorsement of the idea that economic profits are—by and large—justly distributed.
4. The rural bar is more inclined to side with the law rather than with individual rights in those instances in which clashes between the two occur.

5. There is a consistency between the rural sample's support of legal institutions over individual rights and its endorsement of religious institutions as necessary to the moral integrity of the society.

From these overall findings, some theoretical implications suggest themselves. To some extent both the Chicago bar and the rural bar are reflections of their containing communities. Indeed, the liberalism and pluralism found among Chicago lawyers reflect those value characteristics more typical of urban environments. The conservatism and greater consensus among the rural sample tend to reflect the prevailing attitudes of the rural environment. The nearly consistent positioning of the Springfield (urban) data between the extremes of the Chicago and rural data lends support to this contextual notion.

This suggests that the assumption of Goode that a unique set of values will inform a professional group and make it a community within a community is not supported. Rather, what we find is a professional community mirroring a containing community.

In the rural bar there are a number of reasons why this may be so.

1. The vast majority of the rural practitioners are rural products. Sixty-six percent are practicing in the county or in a county adjacent to the one in which they were raised. Their value orientation was acquired in the process of growing up. As Richard Wells (1970:158) suggests, they may very well be captives of the local value systems.
2. Rural law practice is largely entrepreneurial practice. In the rural sample, fully 97 percent practice solo or in two-to-three person firms. Without the shielding influence of a large firm, rural attorneys are directly exposed to the value preferences of their communities. Their success as practitioners is contingent on their reputation in the community. They get clients to the extent that they enjoy the confidence of their community. There is a strong economic incentive to mirror the community's values rather than clash with them.
3. Small communities are intimate. There is little privacy. Public scrutiny is constant. Careers are made and lost over "careless mistakes"—relative to public opinion (Landon, 1985). This scrutiny becomes a discipline, inducing at least nominal conformity with expected standards of thought and behavior.

In light of the foregoing, it is indeed likely that the idea of community does apply to the legal profession in rural settings, but not for the reason Goode suggested. The rural bar is a community because "community" is more nearly the descriptive term for the context in which practice occurs. "Community" carries an implicit discipline for entrepreneurial professions. While rural entrepreneurs may be experts in technical specialties, they are first and last considered to be members of the local community. Their economic survival is in large part contingent on their success in fitting in.

VALUE DIFFERENTIATION WITHIN THE RURAL BAR

One of the primary findings of the Heinz and Laumann study of the Chicago bar was that the value orientations of lawyers in that metropolitan setting vary in a relatively systematic fashion. The researchers found that the practice area in which an attorney works is the most influential factor shaping his or her attitudes and beliefs about value-related matters. This was an additional piece of evidence supporting their overall thesis that the legal profession is differentiated primarily by client interests.

The rural context stands in stark contrast to the metropolitan context for legal practitioners. The opportunity for specialized practice is greatly reduced by the more limited economic environment in small towns. Therefore it is relatively rare to find a small town attorney who is able to restrict his practice to a particular specialty and see essentially only one class of clients. But despite the fact that extensive specialization of practice is not present in rural settings, there is still some modest differentiation in practice patterns. This raises the possibility of examining the variation in values among rural lawyers by some of the same practice variables used in the Chicago study.

One approach to this analysis is to compare rural lawyers with those lawyers in Chicago who are most like them in practice characteristics. Heinz and Laumann (1982:451–52) identified six discrete clusters of lawyers whose clientele and cases tend to distinguish them from each other. These clusters include: (1) large corporate practitioners, (2) regulatory practitioners, (3) general corporate practitioners, (4) political practitioners, (5) personal business practitioners, and (6) personal plight practitioners. Because the client mix in rural areas lacks the variety and richness of the metropolitan setting, it is impossible to identify such clusters in small towns. We are able, however, to generalize about small town practice by looking at the distribution of legal effort in such settings. Table 7.2 suggests that more than 52 percent of all the legal effort in rural settings is focused in only five practice areas: (1) domestic relations, (2) estate, (3) personal injury (plaintiff), (4) real estate (residential), and (5) criminal defense.

Three of these five areas are included in the personal plight sector of the Chicago data. Probate and real estate practice are included in the personal business sector of the Chicago data. Thus, in terms of comparability, the rural bar comes closest to the personal plight bar in the Chicago data, since more than 32 percent of the total effort of the rural bar goes to what Heinz and Laumann define as personal plight cases (see Table 7.3).

Another 29 percent of the rural effort falls under the personal business sector of the Chicago bar. Since the Chicago data do not allow us to construct an exact replica of the general practice content of the rural bar, we must content ourselves with comparisons that are only roughly equivalent.

In order to provide a more general measure of each of the three value dimensions, we have computed the mean score for all the items under each value category. These mean scores are displayed at the end of Table 7.1 as the economic

Table 7.2
Distribution of Legal Effort, Rural Bar

Field of Practice	% of Effort	Cumulative % of Effort
Domestic Relations	15.075	15.075
Estate	13.310	28.385
Personal Injury, Plaintiff	10.995	39.380
Real Estate, Residential	6.690	46.070
Criminal Defense	6.145	52.215
Banking	5.425	57.640
Real Estate, Cmcl.	5.050	62.690
Collections	4.180	66.870
Personal Injury, Defense	3.805	70.675
Criminal Prosecution	3.780	74.455
Commercial, Contracts	3.385	77.840
General Corporate	3.135	80.975
Municipal	2.685	83.660
Agribusiness	2.610	86.270
General Personal	2.440	88.710
General Litigation	2.440	91.150
Taxation, Personal	1.765	92.915
Administrative Law	1.145	94.060
Antitrust, Plaintiff	.750	94.810
Civil Rights	.325	95.135
Taxation, Corporate	.275	95.410
Insurance	.275	95.685
Public Utilities	.200	95.885
Labor, Management	.125	96.000
Environmental	.100	96.110
Labor, Unions	.050	96.160
Other	4.130	100.29*

*Excess over 100 percent due to rounding

Table 7.3
Proportion of Effort Invested in Fields of Practice, Rural Sample

Field of Practice	Percent of Effort	Cumulative %
Personal Plight Sector (Civil rights, criminal defense, divorce & domestic relations, personal injury)	32.540	32.540
Personal Business Sector (General litigation, residential real estate, probate and estate, personal tax)	29.355	61.895
Corporate Client Sector (Business litigation, commercial real estate, business tax, labor-management, utilities, banking, anti-trust, commercial-contracts, personal injury defense, general corporate)	27.800	89.695
Political (Criminal prosecution, municipal)	6.465	96.16
Other	4.130	100.29

Table 7.4
Comparison of Lawyer Value Orientations: Rural Entrepreneurs and Chicago Personal Plight Cluster

Practitioners	Mean Score Economic Liberalism	Mean Score Civil Libertarianism	Mean Score Religiosity Scale
Rural Missouri Sample (n=201)	2.78	2.72	3.14
Chicago Sample (total n=777)	3.23	3.28	2.82
Personal Plight Cluster (n=171)	3.35	3.28	2.66
Civil Rights (n=14)	3.63	3.60	2.64
Criminal Defense (n=44)	3.51	3.56	2.68
Divorce (n=57)	3.26	3.22	2.53
Family (n=27)	3.37	3.10	2.75
Personal Injury (Plaintiff) (n=62)	3.22	3.05	2.66
Generalists (n=86)	3.09	3.10	3.01
Personal Business Cluster (n=165)	3.14	3.00	2.85

Source: Chicago data are from Heinz and Laumann, 1982. Reprinted with permission.

liberalism mean score, the civil libertarian mean score, and the religious values mean score. The scores are computed so that the higher the values, the more liberal the attitudes.

First of all, let us look at the mean value scores of the rural bar and compare them with the equivalent scores of personal plight practitioners in Chicago. By that comparison we can see whether practice type does exercise an influence on value orientations (as Heinz and Laumann's data suggest) or whether other factors such as community context have a structuring effect on attorney values.

Table 7.4 displays the mean scores on all three value dimensions for both the rural sample and the Chicago sample. The data indicate that personal plight attorneys are even more liberal in outlook than the Chicago sample as a whole. Thus the difference between the rural bar and the personal plight sector of the Chicago bar is even greater than the difference between the rural bar and the Chicago bar in general.

This is not a surprising finding, given our earlier analysis of differences between entrepreneurial practice in the city and entrepreneurial practice in the country. But it does add more evidence suggesting that, where practitioners are not insulated from their communities by the existence of highly specialized clientele, their orientations will be less client driven and more community driven.

We can also compare the rural data with the personal business cluster in Chicago since 29 percent of the rural effort is focused on matters included in that sector. The value data in the personal business sector are somewhat more

Table 7.5
Mean Scores, Economic Liberalism Scale, by Practice Area (Rural Sample)

25% or more of Practice Effort in the Field	(N)	Score	Distance from the Grand Mean (2.78)
[2]General Litigation	(7)	3.07	+ .29
[1]General Corporate	(3)	3.00	+ .22
[1]Commercial, Contract	(5)	2.96	+ .18
[2]Personal Real Estate	(11)	2.91	+ .13
[3]Criminal Defense	(12)	2.88	+ .10
[3]Personal Injury, Plaintiff	(32)	2.83	+ .05
[3]Domestic	(50)	2.81	+ .03
[4]Municipal	(5)	2.76	- .02
[2]Estate	(43)	2.75	- .03
[1]Commercial, Real Estate	(11)	2.74	- .04
[4]Criminal Prosecution	(18)	2.71	- .07
[1]Personal Injury, Def.	(12)	2.69	- .09
[1]Collections	(4)	2.55	- .23
[1]Agribusiness	(4)	2.50	- .28
[1]Banking	(10)	2.50	- .28

Chicago Clientele Clusters	Mean Economic Liberalism Score
[1]Corporate Clientele	3.18
[2]Personal Business Clientele	3.14
[3]Personal Plight Clientele	3.35
[4]Political (Govt.) Clientele	3.31

Source: Chicago data are from Heinz and Laumann, 1982. Reprinted with permission.

conservative than the personal plight sector, but still do not approach the conservative character of rural data (see Table 7.4).

We also extracted from the rural data those practitioners who spent 25 percent or more of their practice time in a single area, to see how well the mean economic liberalism score of those practitioners matched the appropriate practice sectors in Chicago. Table 7.5 displays that data. The rural scores are listed from highest (most liberal) to lowest (most conservative). The most liberal scores in the Chicago data are from the personal plight cluster. The rural data, however, show the personal plight practitioners there to be primarily in the middle range of the scores. The most conservative Chicago scores come from the personal business sector. In the rural data, personal business practitioners' scores tend to cluster on the more liberal end of the continuum. Corporate practitioners in Chicago were also on the more conservative end of the scores while in the rural data such practitioners are arrayed on both extremes of the scale.

It does not appear that the client-driven structuring apparent in the Chicago economic liberalism scale data is present in the rural data. Overall, the rural data remain much more conservative and lack any systematic patterning by client interest, even for those whose practices are 25 percent or more in a single area.

DIFFERENTIATION IN CIVIL LIBERTARIAN VALUES

In the Chicago study, variation in civil libertarian attitudes was found to be patterned by practice area and by clientele types, also. Union lawyers, criminal

Table 7.6
Mean Scores, Civil Libertarian Scale, by Practice Area (Rural Sample)

25% or More of Practice Effort in the Field	(N)	Score	Distance from Grand Mean (2.72)
[4]Municipal	(5)	3.20	+ .48
[1]General Corporate	(3)	3.20	+ .48
[2]Agri-business	(4)	3.10	+ .38
[1]Personal Injury, Def.	(12)	3.01	+ .29
[2]Estate	(43)	2.75	+ .03
[3]Personal Injury, Plaintiff	(32)	2.75	+ .03
[1]Collections	(4)	2.75	+ .03
[1]Banking	(10)	2.70	- .02
[3]Domestic	(50)	2.70	- .02
[1]Commercial, Contract	(5)	2.64	- .08
[2]General Litigation	(7)	2.60	- .12
[3]Criminal Defense	(12)	2.60	- .12
[4]Criminal Pros.	(18)	2.53	- .19
[1]Commercial Real Estate	(11)	2.49	- .23
[2]Residential Real Estate	(11)	2.34	- .38

Chicago Clientele Clusters	Mean Civil Libertarian Score
[1]Corporate Clientele	3.22
[2]Personal Business Clientele	3.00
[3]Personal Plight Clientele	3.28
[4]Political (Govt) Clientele	3.18

Source: Chicago data are from Heinz and Laumann, 1982. Reprinted with permission.

defense attorneys, and civil rights lawyers tended to score high on the civil libertarian scale. This should not be surprising, given their involvement with clients who are thought to be struggling against a powerful system. Also showing high scores were elite lawyers working in high-prestige corporate or antitrust work. The lowest scores on the scale were identified with practitioners in the personal business cluster—lawyers specializing in probate, personal tax, residential real estate, and general litigation (Heinz and Laumann, 1982:149–50).

The rural data show no such patterning (see Table 7.6). While residential real estate practitioners have the most conservative civil libertarian scores, other personal business areas such as probate (estate) show scores about the mean. Whereas criminal defense lawyers show higher civil libertarian scores in the Chicago data—presumably indicative of their identification with "downtrodden" clients—in the rural setting such practitioners rank among the most conservative. Ideological orientations presumed to be tied to representing certain types of clients are simply not apparent in the rural data. It is difficult to find any pattern when defense lawyers in personal injury practice have more liberal attitudes toward civil libertarian issues than the plaintiff lawyers representing the "little guy" in the same cases. Likewise, it is difficult to reconcile the attitude of domestic (divorce) specialists working in personal plight matters with an identical score from lawyers working for banks in rural areas.

Part of the difficulty in comparing the rural data with the Chicago data is the fact that areas of specialization are not precisely comparable in the two settings. Moreover, the small cell size of many of the practice areas in the rural data warn one against drawing any dogmatic conclusions. But assuming that corporate and business client interests are significantly different from the interests of individual clients who seek criminal defense or assistance with domestic problems, there is simply little evidence in the rural data that specialized client interests are shaping lawyer attitudes.

ANALYSIS OF VARIANCE OF SOCIAL VALUES DATA

If value differences are not client driven in the rural sample as they appear to be in the Chicago sample, then what accounts for the variation? To answer this question we examined several variables that might be presumed to relate to social value orientations. On the economic liberalism scale, only two variables achieved statistical significance. Political preference showed a statistically significant difference, with Republicans (predictably) reporting more conservative economic values. The second variable to achieve statistical significance was entrepreneurial activity. Those lawyers who operated businesses in addition to their law practice had significantly more conservative attitudes; and the more businesses they operated, the more conservative were their values.

On the civil libertarian scale, none of the variables achieved a level of statistical significance in their difference scores. Religious values were found to be significantly related only to community of origin. The smaller the community, the stronger the endorsement of religious values.

On the economic liberalism scale, background variables such as age, income, political preference, religious preference, and father's occupation together explain 16 percent of the variation in the rural scores. Law practice variables, on the other hand, cumulatively explain only about 6 percent. The significance of this finding lies in its contrast to the Chicago bar data. Heinz and Laumann (1982:154) found that law practice variables alone explained 15 percent of the variation in the economic liberalism scale scores. Within the law practice variables they examined, the field of practice variable was the most powerful, explaining 10 percent of the variance. This gave strong support to their argument that value orientations among attorneys are significantly client driven. The rural data show a considerably different picture. Here, field of practice explains only 3 percent of the variance. This is to be expected given the fact that fewer rural attorneys have anything like the legal specialties that exist in metropolitan settings. Clientele of rural attorneys who do specialize are probably still more diverse than the clients of a corporate law firm in a metropolitan center. The probability of a client-driven value structure among attorneys would presumably decline as the client mix became greater, which is what is found in the rural data.

Also striking is the finding that among the background variables in the rural study, political preference was the most influential factor in explaining economic values. Eleven percent of the variance was explained by that variable alone. In the Chicago study, the background variables model was somewhat different, so we cannot compare the relative influence of political orientation. The most important variable in that model was ethno-religious origin, which explained some 6 percent of the variance. Ethno-religious origin was not used in our rural data since the rural population in Missouri was overwhelmingly white, Anglo-Saxon, and Protestant.

The essential finding of our study is that, among rural practitioners, law practice variables explain little of the total variance in economic values. Background variables (excluding political preference) also explain relatively little of the variance. Thus it appears that ideological orientation in economic values is primarily politics driven, not client driven. The traditional expectation that Republican politics means economic conservatism seems to pervade the rural data.

Scores on the civil libertarian scale leave a relatively ambiguous picture for the rural bar. Background variables explain only 8 percent of the variance, and law practice variables explain slightly less than that amount (7.6 percent). In the Chicago data, bckground variables account for 26 percent of the variance. Using only law practice variables, 29 percent of the variance in scores can be explained. The Chicago data again indicate that ethno-religious background and field of practice contribute strongly to the explanation of variance in civil libertarian value scores. The influence of background and field-of-practice variables in the rural sample are even less important in explaining variance in civil libertarian values than they are in explaining variance in economic values.

CONCLUSIONS

The rural data on value orientations of the bar fail to support the generalizations of the Chicago study. In fact, there was nothing in the Chicago study that implied that its findings should be generalizable over the entire legal profession. But the rural data do serve to sensitize us to the role of context in shaping the ideological outlook of lawyers, as well as their practice patterns.

The impact of context on the economic ideology of rural attorneys appears to be a function of a variety of characteristics of small town practice.

1. Rural America is generally more conservative in economic attitudes, and rural lawyers typically have deep roots in the rural context and a deep commitment to what they perceive to be the virtues of rural life. Therefore, it should not be surprising that their mean score on the economic liberalism scale is significantly lower than that of the Chicago sample. This could be interpreted to imply a client-driven model since rural attorneys serve primarily rural people. But the issue is more complex.
2. Because the majority of clients of rural practitioners are individuals rather than business clients, it is difficult to argue a conservatism driven by a local client segment that, compared with other client groups, is more conservative. It does appear that rural practice is community driven, rather than client driven as in metropolitan settings.
3. The rural context virtually necessitates an entrepreneurial-type practice. The opportunity to be a firm specialist—relying on the firm's expertise and status to generate clients—is not a luxury enjoyed by rural practitioners. The vast majority are solo

practitioners. This means they are simultaneously businessmen as well as lawyers. The economic viability of their practice is a deep personal concern. There is no institutional protection from the harsh realities of economic survival. Therefore, an entrepreneurial ideology is implicit in rural law practice. While legal expertise is required to succeed in the country, a business orientation is equally crucial. Thus, the rural lawyer does not need an array of business clients to shape his ideology in conservative directions. His own survival instincts fuel a more conservative outlook than is likely to occur in a setting where primary attention can be given to a legal specialization, without the responsibility for worrying whether or not the firm will be there tomorrow.

4. The rural context produces a client mix that tends to promote the lawyer's ideological independence. Most rural attorneys have a high-volume business. Their clientele are frequently one-shot clients with only an occasional need for legal services. The probability of becoming beholden to a distinct ideological orientation typical of a particular client group is unlikely. The rural lawyer has to conduct his work so that he continues to draw clients from diverse circumstances. His success is predicated on his ability to continue to generate a high-volume practice. Even if he is able to specialize in a single practice area, most rural attorneys still need the supplemental work that comes from other diverse clientele. Thus, his interaction with clients is likely to expose him to the full breadth of ideological orientations found in the rural context. This broader range of orientations will remain relevant for him so long as an economically successful practice requires a high volume of clients.

The rural data on social values within the legal profession suggest caution in generalizing from the Chicago study that the entire profession's ideologies are client driven. In larger urban contexts where extensive specialization and distinctive clientele groups are feasible, the dynamics are in place to produce significantly differentiated value orientations on the part of lawyers. But in smaller contexts, the requisite dynamics are less likely to occur. One could argue that the more conservative scores on the value scales registered by the rural sample are evidence of client influence, since the entire rural environment is itself more conservative. But the inference in the Chicago study is that lawyers in that setting accommodate their ideological views to those of their special clientele. In the rural setting the evidence suggests that value orientations are acquired in the process of growing up in the rural environment, rather than adapting to the interests and viewpoints of a select client group.

There is no evidence in the rural data to support Goode's notion that lawyers are united by a common set of values and as such are a community within a community. It must be conceded here, though, that neither the Chicago study nor the rural study directly addressed the question of professional values. Thus, the theoretical question of community within a community may need to be more adequately examined. The rural data give little support to Rueschemeyer's model suggesting that business family background and business clients combine to generate a set of business-oriented values among lawyers. In the rural case, it appears to be the rural context that contributes to the greater conservatism. Thus, community context does appear to function as another source of differentiation within the legal profession as a whole.

8

CLIENTS, COLLEAGUES, AND COMMUNITY: ZEALOUS ADVOCACY IN COUNTRY LAW PRACTICE

The issue of professional solidarity has interested scholars for some time (Goode, Merton, and Huntington, 1957; Goode, 1957; Perucci and Gerstl, 1969; Bucher and Strauss, 1961). It has been commonplace to consider professions such as law and medicine to be communities. Practitioners are alleged to possess shared values, a code of professional conduct specifying role behavior toward both clients and colleagues, a shared technical language, and other elements that contribute to a sense of common identity (Goode, 1957).

Most studies of the legal profession have tested this notion and found it wanting (Carlin, 1962, 1966; Ladinsky, 1963; Smigel, 1969; Heinz and Laumann, 1982). Instead of a cohesive "community within a community" as Goode anticipated, the bar has been found to be deeply fragmented, steeply stratified, and constituting essentially a collection of professions so different in background and practice characteristics as to be divisible into entirely separate "hemispheres of practice." Metropolitan conditions of practice are seen to be corrosive to professional community.

The issue of professional community remains intriguing, however, because—as our rural bar data pointed out in the last chapter—there is indeed a certain community to be found among small town practitioners. The question is, what is the source of that community? Is it based in the uniqueness of professional training or is it found in the constraining influence of the containing community?

THE SOURCE OF COMMUNITY IN THE PRACTICE OF LAW

Goode (1957) pictures professional communities as existing within the framework of larger "containing communities." Such containing communities may be as large as an entire society or as small as a local town. The fact that the professional community exists within and in some degree is dependent on a larger containing community suggests the possibility of structural strains between the two communities. In the case of the legal profession, the economic characteristics and the value and normative orientations of the local containing community can very well be imagined to impinge on the professional conduct of practitioners—affecting not only the structure of their practice, but the content and execution of their professional role.

The concept of "professional community" assumes that lawyers are socialized into their professional role in law school and transplant this acquired orientation into a local setting where it will thrive, nourishing and directing their practice of law. There is an implicit assumption that the norms of the profession, rather than the norms of the community, will direct their professional work.

As a matter of fact, this assumption can be much more easily demonstrated in the profession of medicine than it can in law. Community opinions and perspectives will have little impact on a physician who is diagnosing the existence of a strep infection. But the same cannot be said for the way a lawyer defines the issues involved in a civil suit that his client wishes to bring against the local school board and its dress code. Lawyers' work, in contrast to physicians', is inherently ambiguous. Lawyers are licensed counsellors-at-law. But the specific content of that work has never been delineated. The matters that lawyers deal with frequently have their beginning in the unique day-to-day interactions of a given community and remain imbedded in those interactions throughout their resolution. Physicians' work, on the other hand, is highly specified. Ailments are more easily abstracted from their concrete surroundings. The manner in which a disease is addressed by a physician will more directly reflect what he or she has learned in medical school than what he or she has learned about the dynamics of the local community. A doctor's professional orientation can be more easily and successfully transplanted to the practice setting from the school setting than can a lawyer's.

So professions have differing capacities for community, in part because of the differing degrees of specificity of their work, and in part because of the varying degrees to which the issues being addressed can be isolated from the context in which they occur. Even within a single profession, the degree of community may vary. Urban lawyers reflect more fragmentation than community. In addition to the inherent ambiguity of legal work, in urban settings there is a vast array of differing clientele whose legal problems have virtually nothing in common. A lawyer working for a corporation on a securities issue will have little in common with a lawyer defending an illiterate client's social security disability pension in an administrative court.

This chapter then addresses the general issue of professional solidarity within the legal profession. And it asks the question whether, in those instances where solidarity and community do appear to exist, the solidarity is predicated on the assumed *content* of law school training and socialization and buttressed by intraprofessional norms and formal ethics, or predicated on the *context* of practice.

To examine this issue, we will focus on a single dimension of professional conduct: advocacy within the adversarial system of legal representation. The context selected for observation is the small rural community where professional practitioners work under conditions of increased visibility and scrutiny, accessibility, and accountability as compared with large urban settings.

The selection of the advocacy role for specific attention is based on the wide variations inherent in the manner in which that role is executed by lawyers. The adversary process ranges all the way from extreme partisan advocacy (which often is nothing short of combat, employing cunning and ingenious techniques calculated to destroy an adversary, regardless of the factors of the dispute) to "solution-oriented advocacy" aimed at expediting fairness and minimizing combat. Thus, it provides a convenient window through which to observe the possibility of contextual constraints on professional roles.

The primary question to be investigated concerns the interaction between the containing community and professional conduct. To what extent is the achievement of professional community a function of non-professional (local) expectations rather than professional values and norms acquired during socialization and reinforced by codes of professional ethics? Specifically, how is the professional ideal of zealous advocacy modified by expectations of the local community, local clients, and local colleagues in rural communities?

THE RURAL SETTING

The data for the study (as indicated earlier) were derived from in-depth interviews with 201 lawyers practicing in 116 communities within 94 counties of rural Missouri during the nine-month period June 1982 through February 1983. The communities ranged in size from a county seat of 241 inhabitants to two communities of 20,000. Fifty-five percent of the attorneys practiced in towns of 5,000 or less. Forty-five percent practiced in towns between 5,000 and 20,000.

The interviews, lasting from one and a half to three hours, were personally conducted by the researcher in the attorneys' local offices. Observations on the advocacy role of lawyers were woven throughout each interview. It should be remembered, therefore, that our data on advocacy are what we may aptly call "expert opinion"—information offered by attorneys and based on their perceptions of their practice. As such, it lacks empirical verification. It does, however, reflect consensual agreement on the part of the practitioners and illuminates their perceptions of the legal culture within which they work.

The contemporary conventional wisdom about small towns is that the urbanization process has invaded the rural community and has dissolved the bonds of local integration by orienting the local community toward the larger society (Vidich and Bensman, 1968; Martindale and Hansen, 1969). While there may be some truth to this position, its uncritical acceptance is questioned (Richards, 1978; Rubin, 1970). There is simply a lack of evidence to demonstrate that the development of vertical ties between rural communities and mass society has created a corresponding decrease in horizontal ties within communities.

While scholars disagree considerably over the extent and character of the urban-rural distinction, the evidence suggests that the leveling of traditional rural-urban differences—if there has been such a trend—has not progressed nearly so far as some observers seem to think and that "rural and urban differences remain substantial" (Richards, 1970:579). Most research continues to find the rural environment possessing a close sense of community and a pervasive friendliness (Kasarda and Janowitz, 1974; Korte, 1980); a rather fundamentalist religious outlook (Glenn and Hill, 1977:41; Fischer, 1982); a puritanical, prejudiced, and conservative attitude on political issues (Glenn and Hill 1977:41); and sharply distinguishable social attitudes and behavior but an increasingly pluralistic outlook, with most obvious differences being exhibited between farmers and nonfarmers (Fischer, 1982:260).

What is clear is that "rural" and "urban" are points on a continuum, rather than dichotomies. The variations in attitudes, values, and outlooks by community size tend to be monotonic: "The largest communities usually differ from the medium-sized communities about as much (and in the same direction) as medium-sized communities differ from the smallest communities" (Glenn and Hill, 1977:43–44). The evidence also suggests that the attitudinal and behavioral variation associated with community size will not become unimportant as the proportion of rural inhabitants shrink (Glenn and Hill, 1977:50). The diffusion of urban orientations to the country is not so overpowering as is sometimes assumed (Fischer, 1982:50).

Whatever the scholarly debate, people living in small towns presume a significant difference in the rural context and conduct their lives in what they conceive to be a style appropriate to the more intimate environment (Deminoff, 1987). Relationships are more likely to be person-to-person based on friendship than status-to-status based on function. In his work setting the country lawyer toils in a world smaller in scale and infused with familiarity (Bell, 1969:9). Thus there is a tendency for individuals to define themselves as "friends" rather than "clients" when they walk into a local law office. One attorney in a town of 1,800 summarized the feelings of many when he said,

> Here in the country most clients are acquaintances. They come to you as a friend. We've met most all of them someplace before they came to the office—in the lodge, at a school or church function, or in the Christmas parade.

Within our sample of 201 rural attorneys, 43 had practiced in urban settings earlier in their careers. We asked these practitioners to compare their rural and

Table 8.1
How Different Is Law Work in the Country? (in percentages; *N = 43*)

	Significantly Different	Somewhat Different	Not Much Different
How would you characterize rural law practice generally in comparison with practice in an urban setting?	65	16	19
Specifically, in these aspects?			
Content of your practice, e.g., types of cases, clients, etc.	28	40	32
Relationships w/ clients	47	32	21
Relationships w/ Colleagues	56	28	16
Relationship w/ community	74	23	3
How legal matters are handled	42	42	16

urban experiences, first generally and then specifically along five dimensions. As Table 8.1 indicates, the lawyers were decidedly of the opinion that country practice was different. By their description the difference lay less in the content of their practice and more in the manner of their practice and in their relationships. The greatest difference in the content of their practice was the higher proportion of individual clients in the country. What the vast majority perceived to be the most different from what they had experienced in the city was their relationship to clients, community, and colleagues (see Table 8.1).

These data are impressionist on the part of the rural attorneys. They may even be exaggerated. In was clear in the interviews that most rural attorneys possess an anti-urban bias. Some saw large urban firms as ''law factories'' and specialists as ''technicians, not lawyers.'' For the most part, rural lawyers prized their independence and preferred their communities to the ''urban rat race.'' These biases notwithstanding, there do seem to be qualitative differences in law work as practiced in the country.

One of the defining characteristics of country life is the complexity of its social connections. Most persons are involved in multiple-interest relationships. The client who comes to the small town attorney may also serve with the attorney on the local chamber-of-commerce board, or attend the same church, or also have a son on the high school basketball team, or have a cousin who is married to the attorney's wife's niece. Such ''multiplex'' (Van Velson, 1966; Kidder, 1974:11, 31) relationships are quite common in smaller communities and differ significantly from relationships that are more ''simplex'' or single stranded. A simplex relationship would be illustrated by the person who goes to John Jones the dentist for dental work and knows him only in that context and rarely, if ever, encounters him anywhere else. Such relationships are commonplace in large settings.

Multiplex relationships, on the other hand, are commonplace for most people in small communities. This means that their rational ties to others involve a variety of functions and may entail considerable emotional investment. Continual encounters with others are virtually assured, and therefore the motivations that apply to each interactional situation tend to narrow down to those that will make the next encounter comfortable. This attention to amiability appears to be a necessary adjustment to the inevitability of future encounter.

ADVOCACY ACCORDING TO THE PROFESSIONAL IDEAL

Against the backdrop of small town familiarity stands the lawyer's professional obligation, as set forth from 1969 until 1973 in canon 7 of the Code of Professional Responsibility, to "represent a client zealously within the bounds of the law." The U.S. legal system is premised on the principle of "contentious struggle" (Frankel, 1978:21; Simon, 1978:29). This adversarial or "fighting" theory of justice assumes that, through intense partisan conflict, the facts of a disputed matter will be most thoroughly revealed—and a fair decision, made possible (Neef and Nagel, 1974:123).

Lawyers carry the burden of planning and executing the combat, and it is assumed that in an ideal adversary system "the less skilled antagonist will lose" (Frankel, 1978:18). Some have argued that a more sanguine justification for the adversary proceeding lies in the personal gratification of the parties to the struggle, and the gratification is most likely to come through combat (Strick, 1977:109). Whatever the rationale, lawyers are trained in advocacy. It has been said that their most significant professional attribute is their "trained adversariness" (Frankel, 1978:62–63).

The intense partisan orientation of the adversary process has led to abuse. Some fault the system for what it does to the lawyer. It is argued that, since the system requires intensely partisan behavior on the part of the attorney, it sometimes makes tricksters of the bar and could conceivably engender aggressive, combative, cunning, and ingenious qualities in the professional who is committed to prevailing for his or her client (Frankel, 1978:21). As one practitioner has put it: "Law is an adversarial process and its practitioners are not swathed in cotton."

Roscoe Pound argued that the doctrine of contentious procedure "disfigures our judicial administration at every point [and] gives to the whole community a false notion of the purpose and the end of the law" (Pound, 1963:13–14). The process is said to darken rather than illuminate the path of the truth, and thus subvert the intent of the law (Frankel, 1978:53). It is seen by some as a way of processing disputes, but not settling them.

The intensely partisan orientation of the adversarial system, with its focus on individual rights, is also blamed for accelerating social fragmentation (Auerbach, 1976:42). The adversary ethic is thought to epitomize and proliferate antisocial behaviors and is characterized by some as lying at the very heart of the current judicial crisis (Strick, 1977:14).

Most critics of the adversary process advocate its reform—not its abolition—

however (Frankel, 1978:ch. 9; but see Strick, 1977:ch. 15). The abuses of the system have prompted wide discussion in professional circles. One result of the concern and discussion has been that the American Bar Association—after several years of debating a new professional code—on August 2, 1983, adopted a new model called the Rules of Professional Conduct, to supersede the Code of Professional Responsibility. One change, among others, is that the new model rules de-emphasize the adversary principle by defining the lawyer's role as broader than partisan advocacy (Brown and Dauer, 1982:519).

Most studies of the legal process in the United States have been done in urban settings. Illustrations of the alleged abuses of the adversarial process have thus presumably come from observations made in such settings. This raises the question whether the character of the adversary process changes as context changes. More specifically, are there structural differences in smaller settings that affect modifications in the adversary process? Is there an inherent tension between the cohesiveness of smaller settings and strongly partisan representation of individuals in legal matters? Does the limited number of potential clients in rural settings induce a solution orientation to disputes that in other settings might be fought out? Is the high visibility of the rural attorney an inducement to be reasonable—not radical—in the pursuit of remedies? These are typical of the questions that come to mind when one examines the professional ideal of zealous advocacy in light of the small-scale setting and its relationships.

TRIAL WORK IN THE COUNTRY

While the problems handled by rural lawyers cover a broad range of issues, most rural lawyers think of themselves as courtroom attorneys handling litigation. Some do actually specialize in trial work, but as one rural attorney put it, "If you practice in the country, you *are* a trial lawyer."

Trial work creates a paradox for the rural lawyer's public identity. There is a general community assumption that the work of lawyers is trying cases in court; therefore rural lawyers must establish their credentials in large part by their trial work. But the number of trials is steadily declining in the country, according to the respondents. With ever increasing frequency, litigation resolves into negotiation. Nonetheless, lawyers in the country are virtually unanimous in asserting that their public images have been built on their trial work. One lawyer described it this way:

> Here in the country if you can't show that you can fight, not many people will bring their work to you. I don't know whether it is the fact that country folk used to get a lot of their entertainment from court trials or what, but you'd better be able to perform in the courtroom. When I first came here and saw how important that was, I decided to run for prosecuting attorney and get some exposure. I discovered quick and in a hurry that arguing a case before a jury of twelve ends up being talked about all over the county. Those twelve people talk to their friends, relatives and acquaintances and your ability is soon known by everybody.

Despite there being less and less trial work in rural areas, the mystique of the courtroom arena has a deep grasp on rural lawyers. When asked when they most felt like a lawyer, 60 percent replied, "When I am trying a case in court." One attorney revealed the courtroom experience in these words:

> Arguing a case before a jury in the courtroom is for me what speaking in tongues must be for a born-again Christian.

Historical accounts clearly support the perception that the work of lawyers was traditionally done in the courtroom. James Hurst observes,

> Before 1870, both in their eyes and in the common opinion of laymen, lawyers' distinctive business was contest in court. . . . By common consent in the typical community the prizes in reputation, public influence and wealth were due to the able advocate. . . . Men brought business to the lawyer's office when they were ready to fight in court. They expected their lawyers to fight in court. Clients and lawyers carried through to the highest appeal matters which in the mid–20th century were thought too small to warrant appearance in an inferior court. (Hurst, 1950:302)

Part of the appeal of the courtroom lies in its oratory. Historical accounts suggests that "from gossip to oratory, small towns were oral cultures" (Lingeman, 1980:304).

> As sheer spectacle and entertainment, legal trials had it all over vigilantism. . . . People came hundreds of miles to watch the judges and hear the lawyers' pleads. (Lingeman, 1980:121)

A residue of that sentiment persists in small settings in the minds of both townsfolk and lawyers. Many lawyers in the country regularly test the mettle of new lawyers starting their practice in a community by taking them to court on a matter that would ordinarily be settled over the phone. A veteran lawyer confessed,

> Here in the country they want to test you out. There are lots of domestic cases that go to court that could just as well be settled without trial. They're testing the young buck. If you can't stand up in the courtroom everybody will take you there. The way to avoid it is to be good at it.

Despite their apparent preoccupation with courtroom work, rural lawyers tend to agree that litigation in the country is declining. What little evidence we have does suggest that the rate of litigation in the country is less than in urban settings (Daniels 1982; Engel, 1984). A variety of explanations are offered, including higher density of interaction and more role-specific relationships in urban areas (Kidder, 1974:19). But some suggest it may simply be due to the greater accessibility of the state legal machinery in cities (Zemans, 1982:989–1023). David

Engel's (1984) study in rural Illinois discovered that the tight-knit character of the rural community gives people a variety of options for settling disputes short of litigation—including gossip. Residents also cited religion as a source of pacification: It enables them to accept many of life's adversities without resort to suing.

In rural areas the multiplex character of human relationships may also inhibit suing. In contrast to larger settings where people frequently have only one interest involved in a relationship (buying dental services, say, or insuring an automobile), residents of smaller settings typically have many interests involved in a relationship. Two persons may be simultaneously neighbors, members of the same church or service club, patrons of the same local cafe, and parents of children who have established peer-group ties in school. To employ lawsuits in an environment of multiplex relationships is to put too much in jeopardy unless one is willing to risk collapsing a broad network of interests (Macaulay, 1963:55).

THE COMPLICATIONS OF PRACTICE AMONG FRIENDS

In addition to the pervasiveness of multiple-interest relationships the small town conducts most of its affairs within a context of intimacy. A lawyer who had practiced in a firm in a metropolitan setting in Missouri before coming to the country observed that

> Small-firm practice in the country isn't really all that different than small-firm practice in the city. The clients have many of the same problems and you handle a wide variety of matters. The difference is intimacy. In the country you know everybody and everybody knows you. That's where things start to get different.

This is not to say that intimate relationships are peculiar to the rural environment (Fischer, 1982:45–62). It is only to suggest that the small-scale environment in the country, where public familiarity accompanies personal identity, tends to make intimacy more pervasive. One lawyer portrayed the situation this way:

> In a small town, you know everybody, their kinfolk and their histories. The town is like a fabric—you know pretty well how the threads are woven together. You have a mental picture of how the machinery of life operates here, and you get updated every morning at coffee.

Doing legal work within such an intimate environment, and where public scrutiny is constant, creates a level of accountability that probably exceeds that of larger-scale settings. Jerome Carlin's study of solo practitioners in Chicago revealed that it was precisely this kind of limited, scrutinizing environment that small practitioners were seeking to escape (Carlin, 1962:147). In the country there is no place to go. The intimacy of a smaller environment appears to impact the professional's perception of his or her role. Edwin Thomas's (1966:167)

Table 8.2
What Proportion of Your Clients Were You Personally Acquainted With Prior to Giving Legal Service to Them?

Prior Acquaintance with Client	Rural Sample (N=201)	Urban Sample (Springfield) (N=77)
0-25%	4.0	11.6
26-50%	13.0	39.0
50-75%	22.0	32.5
Over 75%	61.0	16.9
Total...........	100.0	100.0

Table 8.3
How Would You Define Your Role as Lawyer in This Community? (percentage of samples)

	Rural (N=201)	Urban (Springfield) (N=77)
Solving technical legal problems................	18.0	26.0
Trying cases in court....	12.0	5.2
Facilitating business enterprises.............	6.0	33.8
Helping individuals......	64.0	35.0
Total	100.0	100.0

comparative study of social workers in agency settings ranging from large cities to rural towns found that social workers in rural settings

1. conceived their professional role more broadly than practitioners in other settings;
2. reflected higher levels of ethical commitment as evidenced through
    a. a more positive approach to clients,
    b. a perception of service recipients as individuals rather than clients,
    c. less social distance between worker and recipient, and
    d. a greater willingness to assume personal responsibility for recipients, along with a compassion for them; and
3. demonstrated a higher quality and overall performance as measured by skill in analyzing problems, appropriateness of treatment plans, and motivation to help recipients.

Our findings are similar to Thomas's work. As Table 8.2 indicates, practitioners in the rural settings were far more likely to be personally acquainted with their clients prior to providing legal service for them than attorneys in the urban setting. Rural practitioners also tended to conceive of their professional roles more broadly than the urban sample did (see Table 8.3). This is due in part to the higher probability of specialization in the urban setting (see Table 8.4). But overall, the rural bar appeared to devote more time to what they called "hand holding" with their clients. Their offices were models of accessibility: Their

Table 8.4
In What Field of Law Do You Consider Yourself a Specialist? (percentage of samples)

Specialty	Rural (N=201)	Urban (Springfield) (N=77)
Criminal defense...........	1.5	3.9
Estate.....................	3.5	9.1
General corporate	1.0	3.9
Municipal..................	1.5	---
Negligence & compensation..	3.0	5.2
Utilities..................	0.5	---
Real Estate................	2.5	3.9
Administrative law.........	0.5	1.3
General litigation.........	8.0	7.8
Banking....................	---	1.3
Civil rights...............	---	1.3
Commercial & contract......	---	1.3
Domestic...................	---	1.3
Environmental..............	---	1.3
Insurance..................	---	3.9
Labor......................	---	2.6
Securities.................	---	1.3
Corporate tax	---	5.2
No specialty	77.6	44.2
Total	99.6	98.8

Note: Totals vary from 100 percent because of rounding.

Table 8.5
What Proportion of Your Time Is Spent in Giving Personal Advice—in Contrast to Legal Advice—to Your Clients?

Proportion of time	Rural (N=201)	Urban (Springfield) (N=77)
0-5%	22.4	42.9
6-10%	27.9	26.0
11-15%	17.4	11.7
16-20%	16.4	13.0
21-25%	10.0	6.5
Over 25%	6.0	0.0
Total..........	100.1	100.1

Note: Totals vary from 100 percent because of rounding.

doors were usually open, with or without appointment. And they spent a considerable proportion of their time in general counseling—about family problems, children's troubles, business difficulties, and moral dilemmas (see Table 8.5).

This helper role is perceived by many rural lawyers as being related to their more diffuse identity in the community. While they are known by the community as attorneys, they are also seen and encountered in a variety of other roles as well. The attorney may operate a local theater or cafe, or be on the church board, or head up the local Optimist club. When a client first comes to an attorney, he often defines himself as "a friend" rather than "a client." Thus the client-attorney relationship is as much person-to-person as it is status-to-status. One lawyer admited his frustration with this ambiguity.

I'm tired of people coming as "friends" taking my time and asking for help but assuming that there will be no charge. I refuse to do legal work on the sidewalk any more. For years, I couldn't go to the Post Office without being stopped by somebody. I tell them now to come to my office. The meter goes on and things go forward in a business-like manner. Some don't like it, but I've got to earn my living as a lawyer.

Most lawyers, however, accept the diffuse identity as a fact of life in small town practice. In many instances it is exacerbated by the lawyer's own pursuit of other business interests in the community besides law practice. In addition to his visibility as town citizen and attorney, he may be known as landlord, farmer, real estate developer, bank director, or shop owner. His broad involvement in the small-scale setting tends to establish his identity as fellow citizen rather than simply lawyer.

The familiarity of the small town also breeds a possessiveness on the part of clients—which further complicates the attorney's work. Some clients expect their attorney to demonstrate exclusive loyalty to them. Failing to understand the separation of professional and private roles, a client may harbor deep suspicions about the friendliness of his or her attorney toward the attorney representing the other side. In most smaller towns, attorneys work with each other regularly, have cordial relations, and are frequently seen drinking coffee together or playing golf. Some clients believe that their interests are being compromised by the congeniality they observe with opposing counsel. If the case comes to blows, such clients worry that their attorney will ease up to retain the friendship of his colleague. Consequently, some will go to a neighboring county for a lawyer "who won't betray them." This demand for exclusive loyalty is so pervasive that one country lawyer tells his clients in the first meeting that "You can hire me to fight your case, but you can't hire me to hate the opposing attorney!"

The perceived intimacy of the small town also raises the problem of privacy and confidentiality in lawyer-client communication. Potential clients, knowing the speed with which information gets around town, may well be anxious about how tight-lipped the office staff is. If they think that their affairs will leak out into the community through the secretary they are again very likely to take matters to an attorney in a neighboring county. Sometimes just being seen walking into a lawyer's office in a small town sets the rumor mill in operation. On occasion, longtime clients and friends will go out of town for counsel for a particular matter simply, as one attorney reported, "because they don't want you to know they've goofed, or are in trouble, or have a problem." Such resorting to strangers to share confidence is not unusual; and in small settings, virtually no one thinks of the local attorney as a stranger (Wolf, 1950:402).

In general, client advocacy in the country is conducted within a framework of perceived intimacy. Clients present themselves as friends, or at least acquaintances, and feel entitled to claim exclusive loyalty from their attorney. They are reported to be uneasy about the apparent camaraderie within the bar and its perceived implications for legal combat. Consequently, it is not unusual for clients to shop out of town for legal services to quiet their suspicions of collusion or allay their anxieties about confidentiality. Overall, the intimacy of the rural setting appears to increase the lawyer's accountability to the client. The relationship between a country lawyer and his client is often multiplex, which adds to the salience of his client's expectations for professional conduct.

LOCAL TRADITIONS AND LEGAL WORK

There are other factors conditioning the advocacy work of lawyers in small settings. Local traditions about legal work exercise a strong influence over the lawyer's practice. In some instances, sizeable towns that have not had local law offices for many years have developed alternative techniques for handling matters that might normally come to an attorney's office. An attorney struggling to open a practice in such a town of 2,500 reported,

> There hasn't been a full-time attorney in this town for 20 years. I thought it would be a good place to set up practice. As it turns out there is a whole generation here who have never used an attorney. They are not accustomed to litigating. For years they have depended upon the Notary Public, the banker, the real estate broker and insurance people for help and advice. I guess they've settled their fights among themselves. The possibility of a law career here is questionable.

In some instances, where communities are quite isolated and people are intimately intertwined by marriage and family ties, disputes do tend to be handled within the family or sometimes by other institutions such as the church. One attorney portrayed the local clergy as playing a prominent role in dispute management:

> Up until the middle 1960's, the priests in this county functioned as judges and juries as well as the law. When I was prosecuting attorney, very few criminal cases came from the —— part of the county. Priests handled matters from the pulpit and meted out punishment in the parish. Virtually nobody went to lawyers. Solutions were fashioned in the parish. The church had a monopoly.

Occasionally the local legal culture has been shaped by a dominant family law firm extending over several generations that has approached its work in a non-adversarial fashion. An attorney in such a firm in a town of 3,000 reported,

> The tradition in this town is to settle matters short of litigation. This firm has been here for two generations and it has never been what you might call "adversarial." If people want to fight, they go twenty-five miles north to —— for an attorney. There hasn't been a jury trial in this town for two years.

On the other hand there are settings that have a long tradition of local trial lawyers whose work is widely known. Local lawyers continue to work in that tradition, and clients seem to accept litigation as an appropriate tool for dispute resolution. An attorney in a town of 7,000 reported that he perceived no general reluctance in his community to using lawyers:

> We have had a long tradition of good trial lawyers here. Some of them have been widely known. The area is used to pretty intense legal activity.

According to the reports of country lawyers, there is an extensive pluralism throughout rural Missouri in attitudes toward using the law. It varies significantly by region—allusions to restraint being more typical of attorneys in smaller communities. But overall there is a general consensus that folks in the country are somewhat more inclined to seek legal redress today than they were in the past. One lawyer illustrated this by referring to a conversation with a client about an assessment dispute on a piece of property that the client had just purchased. The lawyer reported,

> Ten years ago, problems like this were worked out here to the satisfaction of both people. But today I am filing an injunction and the party will sue. People here are simply more willing to use the law than they used to be.

The perceived increase in the use of law may stem from the increased presence of lawyers in rural areas. Only rarely does a community today have only one lawyer in practice, though in the past such a situation was not atypical for many smaller towns. In such one-office towns, law practice is less a matter of litigation and more a matter of mediation. A lawyer in a town of 1,000 observed,

> When I first came here, I was the only lawyer. Because nobody else was around to take the other side, there weren't a whole lot of law suits. As a matter of fact, much of the time I served as a referee. People would come to my office and have at it with each other. Most of the time I didn't have to do anything but listen. If they couldn't settle it themselves, they'd ask me what I thought.

Occasionally, the intimate environment of a small town creates personality conflicts, grudges, and deep-seated hostilities. When these are between lawyers, litigation can be frequent and acrimonious. A lawyer in a small county said,

> Relations between attorneys here are pretty bad. There's too many of us for what business there is. We're on opposite sides of the political fence, too. Elective offices are fought over. I guess it's kind of polarized the county. . . . Coming to an attorney is like choosing up sides.

Sometimes the socioeconomic structure of the community seems to have a bearing on people's decision to litigate. One attorney in a town of less than 3,500 reported that his community was very homogeneous.

People here either work at the shoe factory or for the railroad. Their incomes are very similar. There aren't more than a half-dozen people in town who earn as much as $50,000 a year. People in the same economic situation don't seem to want to take action against each other.

Regional and local variations in legal culture create a mixed picture of the frequency with which people in rural areas resort to litigation. The norm for handling grievances in U.S. society as a whole is direct contact with the source of the problem rather than a trip to the lawyer's office, despite the widely held assumption that people are chronically suing (Miller and Sarat, 1980:525). This norm appears to govern dispute behavior in the country, as well.

There are some issues, however, where one has little opportunity to escape using the legal machinery. Such law-infused matters as probate, marital dissolution, or child custody *require* individuals to resort to lawyers and the courts. But for those matters in which the individual has the option of using a lawyer or not, local customs and implicit social norms impinge heavily on the decision to involve the law. Law use as well as law itself continue to be "mulched in the prejudices and folk ways of the community" (Lingeman, 1980:120). Legal cultures are widely different (Friedman, 1977:ch. 7). Californians resort to litigation about 23 times as often as the Japanese (Henderson, 1982). In Lipay, the Philippines, a festivity without litigation is almost as unthinkable as one without drink (Frake, 1965). In a suburban community of Atlanta, on the other hand, strict Baptists eschew lawyers and courts for conflict resolution (Greenhouse, 1982:17).

The decision to invoke the law in one's personal interest is an extremely complex issue. Zemans (1982:989–1023) has constructed a model for analyzing the decision process on the part of the individual—a model that identifies normative factors, personal attributes of the actor, and perceptual variables associated with expected success and cost of litigating. Recognizing that the U.S. legal system is built on an entrepreneurial principle requiring an actor's decision to invoke legal remedies, Zemans's model makes clear the risks involved in trying to generalize about a class of actors in the country or anywhere else. Nonetheless, our interviews with rural attorneys incline us to agree with Neil Harl that

A residue of sentiment persists in the country that litigation is only a remedy of last resort and entered into even then guardedly and with reservation. (Harl, 1982:9)

REPUTATION AND ITS IMPLICATIONS FOR REPRESENTATION

An additional factor bearing on the conduct of advocacy in the country is the pivotal role of personal reputation. Advertising by lawyers in the country is extensive and efficient, and requires no budget in the law office. It is by word of mouth. Obscurity is not the problem of small town lawyers; they are talked about widely.

As an individual entrepreneur without the cushioning effect of working within a large-scale, broad-based, stable, affluent firm located in a cosmopolitan setting, a country lawyer tends to work on the edge of economic vulnerability. Business-getting involves the meticulous construction and maintenance of reputation. A mistake in judgment in taking a case, mishandling a client, or breaking the trust of a local colleague can have an immediate and telling effect on the attorney's practice.

Seen from the other side, the free publicity given to a lawyer by volunteer publicists is, in effect, a highly efficient means of social control on professional practice. Although the norms guiding the evaluation are local—and not necessarily professional—the accountability is thorough and effective.

The construction of a professional reputation in a small town typically involves more than evaluation of professional competence. The individual is known and known about through the full range of his activities in the community. Many lawyers occupy leadership positions in local institutions, which increases their visibility; many are engaged in enterprises and businesses unrelated to their law work, which tends to color their local identity. The multiple statuses that attorneys have in smaller settings means that reputation-building involves the total community—clients, colleagues, and the general public. The expectations of each of these groups have a high salience for the attorney because each group feeds into the general stream of information that shapes the reputation. With this deeply vested personal interest in appraisal by clients, colleagues, and the community, the lawyer's task is a classic illustration of "impression management" (Goffman, 1959).

THE AMBIVALENCE OF CLIENT EXPECTATIONS

There is a troubling ambivalence in the country. When clients have problems, they want a lawyer who is a fighter—and yet they don't. Lawyers are employed on the expectation that they can win in court if necessary, but still they must not produce a spectacle or make the client look greedy or contentious. That ambivalence drives some clients into neighboring counties for legal representation, as they realize the difficulties at home.

Those difficulties at home again involve the familiarity of small towns. Public awareness of individual conduct tends to be pervasive; consequently there are social as well as monetary costs involved in litigation. During our interviews, many attorneys mentioned the restraining effect of the social costs to clients who had litigable cases. Court litigation is typically alienating (Felstiner, 1974:83). Studies of U.S. legal culture indicate that "litigation is not only incompatible with the maintenance of continuing reelationships, but with their subsequent restoration" (Galanter, 1974:113). The same inhibitions that might restrain a businessman in the city from taking someone to court with whom he must continue to have relations are found frequently in the country in disputes between people (Macaulay, 1963; Engel, 1984). This situation even affects negligence cases. An attorney in a town 50 miles from a major metropolitan center reported a not uncommon occurrence in the country:

> I just settled an accident case in which the plaintiff did not want to sue the other driver because he knew him. It didn't make any difference that the insurance company would pay. He simply didn't want to hurt the friendship. He collected enough just to cover his medical expenses. He was entitled to a lot more.

Another lawyer told of a client in a negligence suit who had assumed that the defendant was an insurance company. When she learned that the defendant would have to be the driver of the other car, she dropped the suit. "I can't sue somebody I know," she said.

The stigmatizing effect of a lawsuit in an intimate environment is frequently cited by attorneys as affecting the decision to sue. Clients draw a variety of inferences about the stigma of litigation. Here are some lawyers' reports:

> People here feel very self conscious about lawsuits. They think it shows greediness and contentiousness.
>
> People in this town don't want their name in the paper as a plaintiff in a lawsuit. They don't want it talked all over town that they are hardnosed.
>
> Solutions rather than suits are wanted here. Town people don't want to be painted as villainous, going around filing lawsuits.

Indeed, there is much about suing and establishing blame that jeopardizes relationships (Zemans, 1982:1024; Hurst, 1981, 401–22; Galanter, 1974; Sarat, 1976; Huntin and Neuworth, 1962:109). In some instances, suits jeopardize reputations, which are an important premise of interaction in a smaller community. In one town of more than 10,000, an attorney told of a person who had a mechanic's lien filed against him. When the filing was published in the local paper, the defendant came to the lawyer in outrage that someone would publicly accuse him of not paying his debts, and he ordered the lawyer to file a countersuit "to clear his good name in the community."

David Engel (1984) cites a prevalent view in rural communities that personal injury litigation is a prostitution of the legal process. In the community he studied, it was assumed that farming is an inherently dangerous occupation and that, if injured, one should take care of oneself—not look to blame someone else and seek damages. On the other hand, abrogation of contract matters in that community were seen as very legitimate issues for litigation. Contracts are made to be kept, and violation of that trust entitles the victim to sue. Such contract suits were found to occur ten times more often than personal injury matters in the local courts he studied.

The visibility and public familiarity of individuals in smaller communities, as well as their local values and multi-stranded relationships, give them reason to reflect seriously on the social costs of litigation. Country lawyers generally believe that people in the country take these costs into serious consideration. The ambivalence created by the desire to protect one's rights while at the same time avoiding the excessive social costs of suing is illustrated by the comment of a client who came to a lawyer with a dispute and said, "I don't want to make anybody mad or anything. And I don't want no big deal all over town. But I have a problem."

The intimate environment appears to constrain the adversarial ethic. The lawyer in the small town becomes the custodian of the client's good name. His manner of proceeding is important to the client. No matter that by training he is a zealot. His clients generally expect him to produce solutions, not fights, and—where possible—conciliation, not combat.

THE SALIENCE OF COMMUNITY EXPECTATIONS

In the work of the small town attorney, the salience of the client's expectations is matched by the salience of the community's expectations because both are primary sources of the publicity that shapes the attorney's reputation.

For most rural attorneys, the local ethos is well understood, and perhaps only rarely reflected on. Sixty-six percent of the rural sample were raised in the county they practice in or in a neighboring county. The local view has been internalized and operates without much conscious deliberation (Wells, 1970:158). But the salience of the local view may be enhanced by an attitude demonstrated when 85 percent of the country lawyers cited leadership in local community institutions as being important or very important to them. Most rural lawyers are deeply imbedded in their communities not only by family heritage, but also by current activities. As the data in Chapter 6 show, 68 percent are active in the local churches; 63 percent are active in local civic organizations; 57 percent have held political office; and 67 percent are currently serving on local not-for-profit boards of one sort or another.

Part of the reason why the opinion of the local community is so important to the local attorney is that his professional aspirations are tied primarily to his local setting. Only 1 percent indicated that leadership roles in the ABA were important to them; only 50 percent indicated that leadership roles in the Missouri Bar were significant in their career aspirations. Whether this simply reflects a realistic assessment of their career possibilities or genuinely indicates their level of aspiration is unclear. In any event, the overwhelming affirmation of the local community as reference group is significant for their conduct.

Small communities themselves enhance the level of accountability of their members through the steady scrutiny given to local affairs. One gets the impression that community size is inversely related to intensity of scrutiny. Thus as community size shrinks, the level of public awareness of local affairs probably increases.

Smaller communities also seem much more able to mobilize a consensus about controversial matters that go on within their boundaries. Because lawyers are often handling troubles—some of which are controversial—they are frequently faced with possible community reactions to the cases they accept (Pollitt, 1964b:43). Reading community opinion about potential cases is not difficult for most small-town practitioners. The community's values and orientations are often imbedded in their own personal-professional judgments. A seasoned attorney in a town of 10,000 said,

> In the early stages of your career, especially if you are not a native to the area, you must be discreet. You will be careful of what fights you take on. You can take more risks later when you have been around long enough for people to know where you stand.

Generally, the risky cases, as far as community reaction is concerned, involve matters that either impinge on the community generally or offend traditional community standards. An attorney in a town of just over 3,500 said,

> I represented a family in a civil rights matter against the school district. It was the worst mistake of my career! The community held that against me for ten years!

Another attorney in a town of less than 10,000 said,

> Recently, I took on a medical malpractice suit against a local doctor. It was a bad mistake. I think I'm finished in this community.

Most of the attorneys agreed that there are clear-cut costs involved in taking on cases the community will resist. A lawyer who grew up where he was practicing said,

> I'll never take on a sexual abuse case in this town. It's one of these matters you quickly refer to an outside attorney.

Reflecting a similar viewpoint, an attorney in a town of more than 15,000 reported,

> People here understand property suits, fence line disputes, damage suits and the like. But they don't understand civil rights mtters. You assess the situation carefully before you take them on.

A practitioner for 25 years in a town of 12,000 indicated that the style of an attorney's work is as important to community response as the content. He said,

> As a lawyer carrying forward a suit in a small town, you don't come across as a tiger and make people mad at you. While you are working for your client, you are also enhancing your reputation in the community. So you try to work quietly and effectively.

Country practitioners seem to agree that community endorsement of their work is an important component in building a reputation and getting business. They do not go out of their way to antagonize feelings in the community, for it happens enough even in the best of situations. As one rural attorney observed,

Law and politics don't mix well. In political life you must be careful not to offend the public. In law practice you must sometimes be a son-of-a-bitch regardless of the public's reaction. In my experience most politicians are poor lawyers.

Reconciling the dual claims of desire for community respect and admiration—on the one hand—and the realistic demands of law practice—on the other—is particularly acute for the attorney who returns to his hometown to hang out his shingle. A young attorney in a town of 5,000 confessed,

The adversarial nature of law practice is perhaps the biggest problem of the rural practitioner, especially when you have lived here all your life. My family has lived here for four generations. Everybody in town knows us, and I know them. They can't imagine my taking action against them. I have had difficulty myself. I found it hard to file a suit. I had to get calloused up before I could accept a lot of work. I had reservations about whether I could be zealous against people I went to church with or had been school chums with. One of my first cases was taking the other side of a matter against a fellow I went to school with and whose mother was a school chum of my mother. They both belong to the same garden club. We all belong to the same church. The family doesn't speak to us anymore and that's hard. Some folks don't care what other people think about them, but I do. I don't know how thick the callouses have to get before you can do this work without cringing.

Sometimes, these "conflict of interest" problems are resolved by referring the matter out of town so as not to make enemies in the place where the attorney needs friends. As the size of the community increases, the probability of this kind of conflict tends to become less.

Ultimately, the attempt to maintain community goodwill and also be an effective leader while practicing law may founder. The inherency of the tension between the advocacy role and the community leadership role is reflected in these observations of a thoughtful practitioner in a town of 5,000 who had struggled to function in both:

In my case, I have just gradually withdrawn from this community leadership role. I think all lawyers ultimately either move toward the citizen role at the expense of their professional role or vice versa. The conflicts must be dealt with sooner or later. In the early years of my practice, to get clients, I tried to be very active in community matters. But in 30 years of law practice I have crossed swords with so may people I feel I have lost all effectiveness as a civic leader. I have just gradually withdrawn and devoted myself to my law practice.

Small town lawyers have a deeply vested interest in promoting the health and well-being of their local communities. Adversarial justice can sometimes be disastrous for the delicate bonds that hold smaller systems together. Jerold Auerbach has argued that "the adversary system with two combatants in every legal ring is ill-equipped to consider the social good, beyond the implicit assumption that every right and any winner is good for society" (Auerbach, 1976:42). Small town attorneys appear to be clearer about the issue of social good, not necessarily because of superior ethical standards but because of the proximity of the health of the local community to their own self-interest. The stability of the community is a precondition for a successful law practice. Rural lawyers are aware of the kinds of fights that can destroy a community from within, such as described by Richard Lingeman:

> Occasionally two leading families would become embroiled in a feud that shook the entire town. In one village the feud boiled over into open economic warfare between the two families, both of whom controlled important businesses in the community, and the family that owned the bank forced the other family's movie theater and hotel into bankruptcy. Demoralization ensued, the baseball team disbanded, the park was unused, business fell off and membership in community organizations plummeted. Even Old Home Week was not held. (Lingeman, 1980:419)

One rural attorney in a town of 2,500 faced such a situation in his practice and observed,

> Lawyers here tend to control their clients in subtle ways, even with tone of voice in order to avoid too aggressive confrontation. For example, we've got a church split here now that has all the makings of a community-wide confrontation. The attorney on the other side and I are trying very hard to cool things down and keep the matter contained. It could blow up the whole community if it got out of control.

Even an attorney in one of the large rural communities we surveyed felt the limits on his role as a zealous advocate:

> I see my role largely as an officer of the court, not a hired gun for the client. I see a larger responsibility to the whole system. In smaller places like this you can quickly see what happens when the system goes out of whack. You are more deeply involved here, so your perspective may be a little broader.

Our interviews revealed that sensitivity to community reactions or social well-being is not a universal characteristic of small town attorneys, however. There is a whole class of attorneys in smaller towns who practice "out" of the community instead of in it. For the most part, they are trial specialists who may handle cases over a 100-to-200 mile radius. They enjoy an immunity to local judgments because they get most of their business from referrals elsewhere. They come closest to being the "hired guns" in rural practice. They have a relatively small stake in the local setting and do not mind taking on matters that would threaten the reputation of a more local practitioner.

Then there are those attorneys who by personality are contentious and combative, but are also local in practice orientation. They are marginals or outsiders in the local bar—porcupines to deal with, and quite indifferent to colleagues' evaluation or community reaction. The local bar establishment has ambivalent feelings toward these so-called outsiders. It sees them as aggressive, combative, and indifferent to local conventions of the "established" bar. But on the other hand, these marginals serve as lightning rods. Aggressive, combative, contentious clients are often drawn to them, to the relief of the other attorneys who wish a quieter and more conventional practice.

In sum, a community's expectation for professional behavior appears to condition the conduct of the local rural lawyer in his advocacy role. Cases are selected with some care. Certain matters are routinely referred out of the community; others may be handled by attorneys whose reputations are already established and run less risk of alienating the community. Some cases go to those who have little stake in the community—whose practices are nonlocal. Occasionally "fringe" lawyers draw matters that others are glad to escape. All these choices and distributions taken together appear to form a clear pattern of case allocation that serves the reputational interests of the lawyer working in a small setting characterized by extensive scrutiny and continuous personal appraisal.

COLLEAGUES AND THE ROLE OF RECIPROCITY

Lawyers in small towns are a relatively intimate community of professional colleagues. They meet regularly as adversaries and often as associates. Unlike those in larger urban contexts where professional encounters with specific other practitioners may be sporadic and occasional, rural lawyers live under the discipline of continuing relationships. One practitioner observed,

> As is true of all small town relationships, [lawyers] cannot and do not deal with each other on the basis they may not meet again. They must and will continue to deal with each other. (Bell, 1969:51)

For the most part, the necessity of continuing relationships means that lawyers make a considerable effort to get along. Already under the pressure of the community's expectation that problems be solved without excessive contention and conflict disruptive to the presumed amiability of small town life, respondents frequently spoke of the additional pressure of preserving collegial ties. One attorney in a town of 4,000 said,

> Attorneys here get along well. That seems to reduce the volume of litigation. No one is trying to make a "loser" out of another lawyer by converting a case into a win–lose situation.

Such a comment is typical of attorneys in the smaller settings who face the inevitability of working very closely with and against each other for years. They are clearly aware that overzealous advocacy can quickly translate into a win–lose situation in court. When disputes are carried into the courtroom for combat, the focus tends to shift from issues to egos. Then it is not so much the case and the client that are on the line—it is the fighter and his ego. One attorney will emerge the winner; the other, the loser. There appears to be an awareness among the intimate little professional group in smaller towns that, in their setting, constant combat—making repeated winners and losers of each other—essentially destroys the fabric of professional relationship. Apparently, in consequence of that awareness, zealous advocacy takes the form of tough give-and-take in solution finding more often than it leads to the clash of combat from which advocates come out either victorious or vanquished. One attorney summarized the matter this way:

> You must carefully modulate the zeal with which you pursue the interests of your client in the country. Too much zeal will alienate other attorneys in the case. Sometimes the client feels that excessive zeal makes him look greedy or abusive. As a matter of fact, if people in a rural area want a fighter, they'll generally go out of town.

However, there are small town settings where the intimacy of the bar produces deep-seated hostility based on long-standing rivalries, grudges, and personality conflicts. A vendetta between local lawyers can turn clients into partisan participants in a larger intraprofessional or interpersonal war.

Occasionally, simple business rivalries such as between two banks in a town will polarize a community and the lawyers along with it. This tends to shade the adversary process toward strong partisanship. But generally, the desirability of good collegial relations among the bar mutes excessive combat, even though there are instances in which the small town setting can become the living definition of contentious procedure.

One of the most pervasive comments we heard from small town lawyers was that the hallmark of law work in the country is informality. Pressed to define what "informality" means, one attorney who had practiced earlier in a metropolitan setting said, "Lawyering in the city is by the book; here in the country it's by *feel*." Another attorney with a similar background said,

> Law practiced in the country is more personal and informal than in St. Louis. Litigation is done by courtesy rather than strict motion and notice.

Further elaboration was provided by an attorney who had earlier practiced in Kansas City:

> City law practice plays by rules which are less accommodating. In the country, attorneys are more trusting and open. They go on the assumption of good will.

It appears that the local legal culture in the country retains some of the heritage of earlier times. James Hurst recalls the conditions that created local standards among professional colleagues.

> In the rural districts between about 1800 and 1870, geography and technology provided the setting for a measure of local bar organization. Settlement was sparse; courts thus must be held at various county seats within a judicial circuit. Travel was hard and dangerous, and lonely; it was natural that the judge and the lawyers should ride the roads together, put up at the same tavern, share the same table. Each little county seat did not yet offer enough business to support a local bar or any sizeable number of lawyers; hence the same group of men, making the common round was likely to do most of the law work through the circuit. . . . Under these conditions there grew a substantial corporate sense in the local bar of rural circuits. There was not only professional fellowship, but also a close sense of what was done and not done. If there was little formal discipline, there was none the less pressure to conform to group standards—pressure that made itself felt in the long discussions and exchanges of professional talk as horses stumbled or wagons bumped their way over the indifferent roads between court houses; pressure that was expressed through the mock courts that were held of an evening at the tavern to call one of the brethren to account for the conduct that day in court. (Hurst, 1950:286)

The precise content of the current local understandings among small town lawyers is summarized in a description given by a lawyer in a town of 15,000.

> You don't have to notice-up for hearings here. Attorneys trust each other—at least until they find they can't.
>
> You don't lay twenty pages of interrogatories on each other out here or run up the bill with depositions. Piling up paper work does not make for good relations in the country. You don't file a five day motion on Charley Jones while he's on a two week vacation, or try to take advantage of him. If he's forgot to file an answer, you don't ask the judge for default. You call him. You pass the case yourself because fairness is more important than winning.
>
> Practice here is on the honor system. The telephone is used instead of paper. We tend to work things out because we trust each other. You soon learn who you can't trust.

The unwritten rules of country courtesy are not left unenforced, though. They are sufficiently important to the professional community that discipline to protect their integrity is swift and explicit. An older attorney in a town of 2,500 said, "If an attorney messes me up, I'll sing like a canary at coffee the next morning." An attorney in a larger community added,

> When an attorney here violates those understandings, the word is quickly passed around. We begin dragging out the interrogatories and imposing the technical rules until the guy gets the message that that's not the way we do things around here.

Yet there are those attorneys in small towns who do not join the club. The difficulty they cause for other more cooperative, reasonable, and trustworthy practitioners has earned them the label of "sons-of-bitches." They are perceived as zealous fighters, masters of tactics, cunning in strategy, abrasive in manner, and "not to be trusted." Because they have abridged the small town attorney-to-attorney role expectations, they are handled differently and scrutinized carefully. Everyone is clear as to who they are. The whole system of legal processing in the country appears to be stabilized by the norm of reciprocity (Gouldner, 1966:136–40). Mutual helpfulness is expected. The formal rules with their specified status duties are laid aside, and an ethos of cooperation is substituted that is less determinant. "Feeling your way along" means that the norm of reciprocity is applied to countless ad hoc transactions between attorneys, each of which is regulated by a shared sense of moral obligation rather than technical rule. In this respect, the norm of reciprocity is

> a kind of plastic filler, capable of being poured into the shifting crevices of social structure and serving as a kind of all-purpose moral cement. (Gouldner, 1966:143)

The rule of informality also suggests that, while a client orientation is clearly present among rural attorneys, it is matched and moderated by a colleague orientation. The self-interest of rural practitioners is not served by an exclusive dedication to client concerns. Most of their clients are one-shot players who may or may not have subsequent business to bring to the lawyer. Colleagues, on the other hand, are important sources of work on a continuing basis (Blumberg, 1967:15). The deep interweaving of kin and friendship ties in a small town means that lawyers face frequent conflicts of interest in cases brought by clients. A local resident may come with a complaint about a piece of machinery he bought from a local implement dealer. The implement dealer and the attorney both serve on the board of one of the local churches. In order to avoid the difficulty of personal ties complicating the resolution of the dispute, the attorney may decide he simply cannot handle it and will refer the client across the street. This happens with considerable frequency in small towns.

Then, too, the attorney representing the other side in a dispute can complicate matters enormously for a fellow practitioner. Rural attorneys work in a high-volume setting where a host of smaller matters occupy their time; consequently, their economic viability depends on the expeditious handling of matters. As noted by the lawyer who was quoted earlier, much of their work is handled by phone instead of paper. They depend on colleagues to cooperate in expediting matters by not demanding a shower of paperwork or showing an unreasonable stubbornness that would require additional hours of time with little prospect of being able to charge the client for them. In this sense, cooperation from colleagues is vital to the well-being of the small town attorney. A practitioner for 25 years said,

> Lawyers protect each other in the country. They will need each others' support over the years since in small town practice the shoe changes foot frequently. If you take advantage of a lawyer's lapses or exploit something that reflects on him, he will get you the next time.

This informality and courtesy characteristic of country practice is essentially professional interaction based on the norm of reciprocity. It expects attorneys to be cooperative, rather than contentious; trustworthy, not tricky; reasonable, not radical. The constant interaction among a relatively small group of private practitioners who can greatly complicate each another's work appears to transform professional relationships. In place of the strong, zealous, partisan relationship of opposing counsel implied in the professional code and governed by a host of technical rules, country practice involves a more person-to-person collegial relationship that is guided by sentiment—not written rules—and that accommodates the self-interests unique to practitioners in small settings. The essential identity among colleagues is personal, rather than formally professional. The country practitioner claims that this results in efficiency: Less gets litigated; more gets solved. And the professional community remains intact.

ACCOUNTABILITY AND ACCOMMODATION

The legal profession as a whole continually faces the vexations of a poorly articulated role set (Merton, 1957:368). Lawyers are designated as officers of the court with responsibility to promote the cause of justice. They are advocates of their clients' interests, and obligated to pursue them zealously. They are colleagues of opposing counsel and expected to conduct themselves with appropriate respect for other members of the professional family. And they are public servants, called to serve the public good. In many instances the obligations inherent in one role make it difficult—if not impossible—to fulfill the obligations of another role. For example, it is unlikely that an attorney would tell his or her client that, while the case itself is just, the social consequences stemming from its successful prosecution would not be in the collective good, and that therefore the case must be abandoned. Charles Curtis has noted the same inherent tension between the lawyer's roles as an officer of the court and as a partisan advocate.

> [The] relations which a lawyer has with his client on one hand and his court on the other are somewhat bigamous. (Curtis, 1954:20)

The resolution of these inherent conflicts usually occurs in favor of the client, whose claims on the attorney for partisan advocacy are backed up by economic rewards. The existing professional orientation seems to tilt toward the attorney as zealous partisan in adversarial matters. And perhaps, in most instances, the lines of lawyer accountability run most directly and most immediately to the client. This being so, it is not difficult to imagine how in some settings balancing all the supposed obligations to the court, the community, and colleagues may have less salience—and how the imbalance may allow abuse of the adversarial ideal to develop.

But in the small town setting, the context is somewhat different. Here, not only do the lines of accountability run to the client with considerable directness—they also run to community and colleagues with somewhat equivalent directness. One practitioner in the country who had previously practiced in a large city said,

In the city, the solo practitioner is accountable to no one! Here in the country you are accountable to *everyone*!

The observation may be distorting because of its exaggeration, but it correctly conveys the sense of accountability that is associated with practicing law in small places.

The unique thing about accountability in the country is its multifaceted character and its evenness in salience. Accountability to the client is predicated on the fiduciary relationship and strengthened by the multiple ties that frequently bind client to practitioner. The practitioner is clearly aware that he cannot afford to have a client bad-mouthing him in a small town. Accountability to colleagues is raised to a very salient level by their ability to facilitate or frustrate a high-volume practice. Dependent on them in some instances for referrals—and in all instances for not obstructing reasonable solutions to clients' problems—the country practitioner cannot afford to conduct his practice as if he may never encounter a particular colleague again. Accountability to the community is raised to a very salient level because reputation is the individual entrepreneur's chief business-getting tool. This tool is forged in the community. And the smaller community—with its intense scrutiny and discussion of its members' conduct, and its greater ability to mobilize consensus about controversial matters (including clients and cases)—becomes a formidable source of sanctioning. In combination, these varying centers of appraisal and accountability constitute a substantial reference system for legal practice.

What becomes apparent is that the expectations of the local setting—clients', colleagues', and community's—are relatively well articulated together, at least in regard to the issue of partisan zeal. Clients in the country (with some exceptions) tend to prefer solutions, not confrontations; they prefer low-key advocacy, not the clash and clang of combat. Colleagues certainly expect balance and reasonableness from opposing counsel, an absence of sharp practices and advantage-taking, and partisanship but not contentiousness. The community expects the avoidance of divisive and offensive issues. While individual interests are important, they are not to be pursued at the expense of the community or its valued amiability.

The convergence of these expectations at the community level impinge on the execution of the lawyer's role at the professional level. Excessive zeal becomes deviance. Thus, while the rural lawyer's conduct may be informed by the professional code, it is ultimately shaped by the day-to-day necessities implicit within the containing community.

The sense of our conversations with the rural attorneys was that they *are* a professional community. But their shared orientation, values, and manner of proceeding are less rooted in their professional training than in their local setting, at least so far as zealous advocacy is concerned. The adversary ethic on which the U.S. legal system is predicated and into which the lawyer becomes systematically trained in law school becomes redefined under the practicalities of entrepreneurial practice in intimate settings. The role of the rural attorney emerges as a unique partisanship—an advocacy shaped by a generally conservative clientele, a pervasive accountability to the local community, and a deep interdependence among local professional colleagues.

9

CONCLUSION: THE BAR AS AN EXTERNALLY DETERMINED SOCIAL SYSTEM

The bar is clearly not a monolithic, well-integrated professional community. It has the appearance of a multiplicity of professions, separated into independent spheres of activity and sharing only superficial commonalities. The most current analysis of this fragmentation suggests that client interests, ethno-religious backgrounds, and politics are the primary influences differentiating and organizing the bar (Heinz and Laumann, 1982).

It has been the argument of this study of the rural bar that, indeed, the legal profession is an externally determined social system. Furthermore, we have argued, there is a prior source of external structuring that precedes the client influence so much in evidence in Chicago. We have suggested that community context is the prior organizing principle. The scale, character, and quality of local economic, social, and political institutions along with certain demographic characteristics create a context that eventually bestows the observed differentiation on the legal profession. We have attempted to illustrate that argument of analyzing the bar in two extremely different settings: the metropolitan and the rural.

The characterization of the legal profession as an externally determined social system finds strong support in the rural bar. The homogeneity of the rural bar, the entrepreneurial practice style, the commonality of clients and cases, the close consensus on values, and the muting of zealous partisan advocacy are all demonstrated to be adaptations to the realities of the small town context. The essential solidarity and community of the rural bar arises less from internal professional values and principles than it does from the external forces that press upon it. Its solidarity is rooted in the same source as the metropolitan bar's diversity: the community context.

The metropolitan bar is impacted by ethno-religious variations because the metropolitan setting studied (Chicago) is ethnically diverse, in contrast to the more homogeneous rural setting. The bar is a ready source of upward mobility for individuals in any setting—rural or metropolitan. In rural areas, the sons of professionals, administrators, blue-collar workers, and farmers may all aspire to law careers. The difference is that, in the rural setting, the ethnic background of the blue-collar family is rarely different from the professional or managerial or farm family. But in the metropolitan setting, ethnic diversity is the norm. It has already structured many parts of urban life. For one thing, a screening system is already in place that channels certain aspiring lawyers to prestigious full-time national law schools. The channeling system directs others to part-time or night proprietary law schools—which starts the inevitable constriction of opportunity for that segment of the bar.

The heterogeneity of the metropolitan setting creates the context for the development of an ethnic bar, a stratified profession, and a moral division of labor. The homogeneity of the rural context, on the other hand, generates a homogeneous bar—minimally stratified, and practicing with a relatively common client mix. This homogeneity resists the emergence of a moral division of labor. The immense size of the metropolitan setting creates the possibility for specialized practice. Both the variety and the number of clients make it possible to restrict practice to certain client types, whether they be prestigious corporations and their elite managers or else modest individuals bringing a variety of personal plights ranging from divorce and personal injury problems to the need for criminal defense. The very limited size of the small town precludes such specialization. There are not enough clients in a single classification to enable an exclusive practice. So all attorneys have a variety of clients. Client interests can structure the legal profession in metropolitan settings because the context enables a limiting of practice to specific clientele. Client interests cannot structure practice in rural settings because the client load is, by necessity, diverse. Some corporate practice does combine with some small business practice to form an amalgam that hardly possesses a set of unique client perspectives and interests. It is not surprising that client interests are the primary differentiating factor in the metropolitan bar, and are not the primary structuring influence in the rural bar. The role of client interests is a function of the prior structuring effect of the community context.

By describing the legal profession as an externally determined social system, attention is being called to the fact that the profession is structured more by its environment than by its unique professional code or its arcane knowledge. The uniqueness of the legal profession lies in the fact that its roots are inevitably thrust into the soil of the social and economic life of a given local community. That soil varies as communities vary. There will be no corporate practice where corporations do not exist. Patent attorneys will not practice where inventions are unlikely. The practicing bar in a resort community will have different experiences from the bar in a farming community. Medical malpractice suits are unlikely to occur where only one physician practices. Labor law will not be practiced where unions do not exist. Personal injury practice may be unlikely in Sander County (Engel, 1984) while very likely in Cook County.

Unlike the profession of medicine, which practices in a relatively fixed realm of disease and trauma, law is practiced in a fluid realm of human interaction. While the territories of interaction to which the law applies are generally known, the precise context of law practice is revealed only as the local economic and social institutions interact to shape the agenda for the attorney. It is not remarkable that law practice in large cities follows the contours of metropolitan life in its diversity and dynamics. Nor is it remarkable the country law practice mirrors its local milieu. It is not legal theory alone that organizes the legal profession: It is also local context.

Nowhere is this ecology of law practice more apparent than in the experience of solo practitioners in our two contrasting settings. Lawyers on their own in metropolitan settings are escorted by the character of their setting into being marginal professionals while their rural colleagues become core practitioners in their setting. The professionally stratifying forces of the metropolitan setting create a moral division of labor that describes the urban solo attorney's practice as "dirty work" and "residual." Essentially the same type of practice in the country is seen as normative, not derogative. Entrepreneurial practice in the city is an adaptation to the harsh realities of a very competitive system. It is probably not the place to which a young lawyer aspires in the beginning. In the country, entrepreneurial practice is not just *a* form of practice; it is *the* form. It is not adaptively accommodated. It is deliberately sought. All these contrasts are constructed out of the materials of context. Not only does the community context shape the contours of practice, but it assigns meaning to them as well; and the meanings vary from setting to setting.

The city entrepreneur adapts to the urban setting by a heavy reliance on brokers for business. The rural entrepreneur relies on reputation. The urban entrepreneur struggles with anonymity, but enjoys immunity. Finding it hard to be known in the midst of the mass, the urban entrepreneur turns to brokers. An unhappy client is of little concern, since the dissatisfied are unlikely to be able to steer very many others away from the attorney. The rural entrepreneur—on the other hand—enjoys familiarity and visibility, but struggles with the accompanying accountability. He has to be concerned about client satisfaction since he relies on reputation for business. Again, we see how the context structures the experience and therefore the practice characteristics of the attorney.

We also found that rural attorneys adapt their evaluation of the various practice areas to the logic inherent in the local setting. Where clients are numerous enough to facilitate specialization of practice, a client-driven structure of deference is found. High-prestige practice areas are those associated with high-prestige clients. But in the rural setting, such a logic is not feasible because exclusive practices rarely exist. In its place is the income-driven structure of deference. Status in rural practice is difficult to achieve along client lines since nearly every lawyer has a client mix that defies categorical description. So lawyer income becomes the differentiating principle for the rural entrepreneurial bar. Those practice areas that are financially most lucrative are seen as prestigious. So even the structure of deference has a logic adapted to the contours of context.

ACHIEVEMENT OF PROFESSIONAL COMMUNITY IN THE COUNTRY

The metropolitan bar is portrayed as highly differentiated—a deeply fragmented professional community. The rural bar, on the other hand, reflects a certain solidarity—a homogeneity of values, backgrounds, practice characteristics, and professional roles. Our study suggests that the fragmentation of the metropolitan bar and the observed solidarity of the rural bar are rooted in the same source: the containing community. Observers of metropolitan law practice suggest that

> intraprofessional concerns, motivations, and interests count for very little in the social structure of the profession. All of the organizing principles that appear to have the greatest influence—client demand, ethnoreligious origin and politics—arise outside the profession. (Heinz and Laumann, 1982:354)

In the metropolitan case, the source of professional fragmentation is found in the heterogeneity of the containing community.

The rural bar is as susceptible to external structuring as is the metropolitan bar. The difference is that in the rural case the containing community is more homogeneous, which produces a mirroring homogeneity in the profession.

Intraprofessional concerns, motivations, and interests are no more salient in the rural bar than they are in the metropolitan bar. But the explanation for this fact differs. In the rural bar the numbers of practitioners in a single community are relatively small. In the smallest settings there are frequently only one or two attorneys. Even in the larger settings, the numbers rarely exceed 15 or 20. Thus the rural bar lacks the critical mass necessary to make the bar a viable professional entity at the local level. It typically organizes itself—if at all—on the judicial circuit level, rather than locally. Circuit bar activities are reputed to be primarily social in focus, not professional. In the rural context, the organized bar's capacity to reward, recognize, and enhance the status of its members is limited. Consequently the level of interest in and concern for intraprofessional activities is minimal.

In the rural bar, the community is the primary structuring influence. This is so for a number of reasons. First of all, the community is the most viable source of recognition and reward for the lawyer. It is more status enhancing to be recognized as a community notable in a town of 5,000 than it is to be recognized as an able lawyer by a professional community of seven attorneys. Furthermore, rural lawyers recognize that the economic viability of their containing community has significant implications for the success of their own practice. Therefore, given the option of involvement in intraprofessional concerns or community concerns, the rural lawyer is going to choose the latter as a matter of self-interest. Rural lawyers come close to illustrating Talcott Parsons's (1951:434–73) notion of professions showing a "collectivity orientation"—a dedication to the commonweal. But the rural bar reflects this collectivity orientation not because it suppresses "self-regard"—as Parsons assumes—but precisely because its own interest lies in being dedicated to the commonweal in small settings.

As our data have indicated, business-getting practices in the small rural community further require the lawyer to be accountable to his context. Entrepreneurial practice in the country is predicated on community reputation. The rural practitioner does not enjoy the relative anonymity of the metropolitan entrepreneur, whose practice is immersed in the vastness of a large setting. By contrast, the rural practitioner works in an environment of visibility and continuing scrutiny. He carefully crafts a reputation for being competent, concerned, helpful, and loyal. That reputation is the magnet that draws clients to his door. The community is the context in which that reputation is gained and lost. His attachment, then, to the community is an adaptation to the realities of small town practice.

While it is true that the centrifugal forces operating in the metropolitan bar are not present in the rural bar, it is not true that the resulting solidarity experienced by the rural bar is based on intraprofessional forces including law school socialization and professional associations. Rural lawyers are not disaggregated by practice specialization as their metropolitan colleagues are. But neither are their internal sources of solidarity any match for the external structuring forces of the community. We observed, for example, that the power of the internal code requiring the lawyer to be a zealous partisan advocate for the client was reshaped under the external influences of community, clients, and colleague needs for efficient handling of cases. We observed also that the value orientations of attorneys on economic, civil libertarian, and religious issues were more tuned to the contours of the rural tradition than to some singular set of client interests.

In sum, the rural bar is not insulated from the community by an exclusive client set whose unique values and interests would influence the attorneys' own positions on issues. Rather, they are practitioners who stand very visible and very accountable to their community and adapt their practice to those realities. The resultant professional solidarity is more apparent than real. It is driven by the community—not by exclusive client groups as is the case in Chicago, nor by intraprofessional sources as was supposed by Goode (1957).

THE QUALITY OF JUSTICE IN THE RURAL COMMUNITY

The hallmark of rural law practice is its accountability. The small town practitioner is a member of a community that celebrates the visibility of its citizens and operates on the premise of familiarity. In the small town this more intimate community is not an option to be chosen—it is generally imposed on everyone, whether they like it or not. For the attorney, this means that he and his practice are part of the public landscape—viewed and scrutinized by virtually everyone! Such intense public scrutiny is two sided. It provides the basis on which a reputation can be built, which assures a successful practice. It also provides the basis on which one can be professionally undone in record time.

This high level of accountability embraces all small town attorneys. There is no exempt class. There is no sector of the bar that serves a special clientele who will insulate it from community scrutiny and judgment. There are—as mentioned in earlier chapters—a few attorneys here and there who successfully practice outside this system. They may represent insurance companies and work cases over a relatively wide area—which would separate them from practicing on a continuing basis in any local community. Or they may simply be "outsiders"—practitioners who refuse to accept the local conventions and are able to find enough clients who share their marginal position. But for the most part, rural lawyers are distinguished by their accessibility and the degree of their accountability. This means that nearly everyone in the professional community operates under the same system and is sensitive to the same scrutiny. There is not, at least along this dimension, a stratification of legal services into multiple systems of justice. Virtually all are held accountable to the same standards, work within a common system, and provide services to a similar range of clients.

Whether this absence of hierarchy in the rural bar guarantees a high quality of legal service in rural areas may be questioned. We have no evidence to suggest that rural lawyers do better or less well in law school than their urban counterparts. We do know they are less likely to have attended prestige law schools. But that is not surprising, given the fact that relatively few lawyers attending prestige law schools market their enviable educational credentials as entrepreneurs. Most of them have their eye on institutional practice settings where elite clients and elite colleagues are the norm. The rural data suggest that nearly all rural entrepreneurs are educated in academically sound institutions. Less than 1 percent were educated in proprietary law schools. More than 90 percent went to law school full-time during the day. Rural practitioners are thus distinguished from the metropolitan bar, 45 percent of whom received their education from fourth-tier (local) law schools in Chicago (Heinz and Laumann, 1982:445). In fact, of those Chicago lawyers whose clients are most likely to be individuals, 64 percent took their training in local schools. Such background characteristics and other differences between lawyers representing individuals and lawyers representing corporate clients led Heinz and Laumann to conclude that such a "hierarchy of lawyers suggests a corresponding stratification of law into two systems of justice, separate and unequal" (1982:385).

No such hierarchy of practice exists in the rural setting. This would suggest that individuals in rural settings may well be served more adequately than most individuals in metropolitan settings. Individuals remain at the core—not the periphery—of rural law practice. They are not a residual category of clients relegated to a segment of the bar who are unable to get access to more powerful and distinguished clientele.

Again, the fact that individuals in the country may receive higher quality legal services than many individuals in larger settings receive does not necessarily mean that rural attorneys are more dedicated to the needs and interests of individuals. It simply means that the constraints of context do structure the delivery of legal services as surely as they structure practice type, professional role, and partisan advocacy.

Overall, the evidence from both the rural data and the metropolitan data suggest that the legal profession is adaptive in its relationship to its environment. The forces organizing the work of the practitioner as well as his relationship to his clients, colleagues, and community are primarily external. This fact suggests that an ecological approach to professional practice is a promising line of inquiry.

REFERENCES

Abbott, Andrew (1981). Status and Status Strain in the Professions. *American Journal of Sociology, 86,* 819–35.

——— (1983). Professional Ethics. *American Journal of Sociology, 88,* 855–85.

Auerbach, Jerold S. (October 1976). A Plague of Lawyers. *Harpers Magazine,* 42.

Bell, Thomas Reuben (1969). Law Practice in a Small Town. Unpublished Masters thesis, Harvard University Law School.

Bellah, Robert N., Richard Madsen, William M. Sullivan, Ann Swidler, and Steven Tipton (1985). *Habits of the Heart.* Berkeley: University of California Press.

Bender, Thomas (1975). *Toward an Urban Vision: Ideas and Institutions in 19th Century America.* Lexington: University Press of Kentucky.

Blumberg, Abraham S. (1967). The Practice of Law as a Confidence Game: Organizational Cooptation of a Profession. *Law and Society Review, 1,* 15.

Bollens, John C. and Henry J. Schmandt (1982). *The Metropolis.* New York: Harper and Row.

Bradshaw, T. K. and E. J. Blakely (1979). *Rural Communities in Advanced Industrial Society.* New York: Praeger.

Bromall, Irvin (1968). Lawyers in Politics: An Exploratory Study of the Wisconsin Bar. *Wisconsin Law Review,* 751–65.

Brown, Louis M. and Edward Dauer (1982). Professional Responsibility in Non-adversarial Lawyering: A Review of the Model Rules. *American Bar Foundation Research Journal,* 519.

Bucher, Roe and Anselm Strauss (1961). Professions in Process. *American Journal of Sociology, 66,* 325.

Carlin, Jerome E. (1962). *Lawyers on Their Own: A Study of Individual Practitioners in Chicago.* New Brunswick, N.J.: Rutgers University Press.

——— (1966). *Lawyers' Ethics: A Survey of the New York City Bar*. New York: Russell Sage Foundation.

Carlson, J. E., M. L. Lassey, and W. R. Lassey. (1981). *Rural Society and Environment in America*. New York: McGraw-Hill.

Carniero, R. L. (1967). On the Relationship between the Size of Population and Complexity of Social Organization. *Southwest Journal of Anthropology, 23*, 234–42.

Carroll, Glenn R. (1984). Organizational Ecology. *Annual Review of Sociology, 10*, 71–93.

Carr-Sanders, Alexander Morris (1955). Metropolitan Conditions and Traditional Professional Relationships. In Robert Moore Fisher (ed.), *The Metropolis in Modern Life*. Garden City, N.J.: Doubleday.

Cheatham, E. E. (1938). *Cases and Materials on the Legal Profession*. Chicago: Foundation Press.

Clemente, Frank and Richard A. Sturgis (1978). The Division of Labor in America: An Ecological Analysis. *Social Forces, 51*, 176–82.

Cohen, Michael (1966). Law and Public Office Holding: A Study Comparing Political and Non-political Lawyers. Unpublished Ph.D. dissertation, Cornell University.

——— (1969). Community Size and Participation by Lawyers in Community Politics. *Journal of Politics, 31*, 1107–10.

Coleman, James S. (1982). *The Asymmetric Society*. Syracuse: Syracuse University Press.

Cornman, John N. and Barbara Kincaid (1984). *Lessons from Rural America*. Cabin John, Md.: Seven Locks Press.

Cozzens, James G. (1937). *By Love Possessed*. New York: Harcourt, Brace.

——— (1965). *The Just and the Unjust*. New York: Harcourt, Brace.

Curran, Barbara A. et al. (1985). *The Lawyers' Statistical Report: A Statistical Profile of the U.S. Legal Profession in the 1980s*. Chicago: American Bar Foundation.

Curtis, Charles (1954). *It's Your Law Too*. Cambridge, Mass.: Harvard University Press.

Daniels, Stephen (1982). Civil Litigation in Illinois Trial Courts: An Exploration of Rural–Urban Differences. *Law and Policy Quarterly, 4*, 190.

Deminoff, William, ed. (1987). *The Small Town in America*. Proceedings of a symposium held March 4–7, at Grinnell College, Grinnell, Iowa.

Derge, David R. (1959). The Lawyer as Decision-maker in the American Legislature. *Journal of Politics, 21*, 408.

Dillman, D. A. and D. J. Hobbs, eds. (1982). *Rural Society in the U.S.: Issues for the 1980s*. Boulder, Colo.: Westview Press.

Dos Passos, John R. (1907). *The American Lawyer: As He Was—As He Is—As He Can Be*. New York: Banks Law.

Duncan, Otis T. (1961). Community Size and the Rural–Urban Continuum. In Jack Gibbs (ed.), *Urban Research Methods*. Princeton, N.J.: Van Nostrand.

Duncan, Otis T. and Albert J. Reiss, Jr. (1950). *Social Characteristics of Urban and Rural Communities*. New York: Wiley.

Duncan, Otis T., W. Richard Scott, Stanley Leiberson, Beverly Duncan, Hal Winsborough (1960). *Metropolis and Region*. Baltimore: Johns Hopkins University Press.

Engel, David M. (1980). Legal Pluralism in an American Community: Perspectives on a Civil Trial Court. *American Bar Foundation Research Journal*, 425.

——— (1984). The Ovenbird's Song: Insiders, Outsiders, and Personal Injuries in an American Community. *Law and Society Review, 18*, 551.

English, William F. (1947). The Pioneer Lawyer and Jurist in Missouri. *University of Missouri Studies, 231,* 2.

Engstrom, Richard L. and Patrick O'Connor (1980). Lawyer-Legislators and Support for State Legislative Reform. *Journal of Politics, 42,* 267–76.

Erlangler, Howard S. (1980). The Allocation of Status within Occupations: The Case of the Legal Profession. *Social Forces, 58,* 882–903.

Eulau, Heinz and John D. Sprague (1964). *Lawyers in Politics: A Study in Professional Convergence.* Indianapolis: Bobbs-Merrill.

Felstiner, William L. F. (1974). Influences of Social Organization on Dispute Processing. *Law and Society Review, 9,* 63–89.

Fischer, Claude S. (1976). *The Urban Experience.* New York: Harcourt, Brace, Jovanovich.

——— (1982). *To Dwell among Friends: Personal Networks in Town and City.* Chicago: University of Chicago Press.

Ford, Thomas R., ed. (1978). *Rural USA: Persistence and Change.* Ames: Iowa State University Press.

Frake, Charles O. (1965). *Litigation in Lipay: A Study of Subanum Law.* Proceedings of the Ninth Pacific Scientific Congress, 1963. Quoted in Laura Nader, The Anthropological Study of Subanum Law (Part II). *American Anthropologist, 67,* 3–21.

Frankel, Marvin E. (1978). *Partisan Justice.* New York: Hill and Wang.

Freidson, Eliot (1972). *Profession of Medicine.* New York: Dodd, Mead.

Friedman, John and John Miller (1965). The Urban Field. *Journal of the American Institute of Planners, 31,* 312–20.

Friedman, Lawrence M. (1973). *A History of American Law.* New York: Simon and Schuster.

——— (1977). Legal Culture. In *Law and Society: An Introduction.* Englewood Cliffs, N.J.: Prentice Hall.

Galanter, Marc (1974). Why the "Haves" Come Out Ahead: Speculations on the Limits of Legal Change. *Law and Society Review, 9,* 95–113.

——— (1983). Mega-law and Mega-lawyering in the Contemporary U.S. In Robert Dingwall and Philip Lewis (eds.), *The Sociology of the Professions.* New York: St. Martin's Press.

Glenn, Norval D. and L. Hill (1977). Rural and Urban Differences in Attitude and Behavior in the U.S. *Annals of American Academy of Political and Social Sciences, 429,* 36.

Gluckman, Max (1955). *The Judicial Process among the Barotse of Northern Rhodesia.* Manchester, England: University Press for the Rhodes-Levingston Institute.

Goffman, Erving L. (1959). *The Presentation of Self in Everyday Life.* Garden City, N.Y.: Doubleday.

Goldstein, Marshall N. (1964). Political Involvement among American Law Students. Unpublished Ph.D. dissertation, University of North Carolina.

Goldthorpe, John H. and Keith Hope (1972). Occupational Grading and Occupational Prestige. In Keith Hope (eds.), *The Analysis of Social Mobility: Methods and Approaches.* Oxford, England: Clarendon Press.

Goode, William J. (1957). Community within a Community: The Professions. *American Sociological Review, 22,* 194–200.

Goode, William J., Robert Merton, and Mary Jean Huntington (1957). *The Professions in Modern Society*. New York: Russell Sage Foundation.

Gouldner, Alvin W. (1966). The Norm of Reciprocity: A Preliminary Statement. In Bruce Biddle and Edwin J. Thomas, *Role Theory: Concepts and Research*. New York: John Wiley and Sons.

Green, Justice J., John R. Schmidhauser, Larry L. Berg, and David Brady (1973). Lawyers in Congress: A New Look at Some Old Assumptions. *Western Political Quarterly, 26*, 440–52.

Greenhouse, Carol J. (1982). Nature Is to Culture as Praying Is to Suing: Legal Pluralism in an American Suburb. *Journal of Legal Pluralism and Unofficial Law, 20*, 17.

Gutterman, S. S. (1969). In Defense of Wirth's "Urbanism as a Way of Life." *American Journal of Sociology, 74*, 492–99.

Hain, Paul L. and James E. Pierson (1975). Lawyers and Politics Revisited: Structural Advantages of Lawyer-Politicians. *American Journal of Political Science, 19*, 41–51.

Handler, Joel F. (1967). *The Lawyer and His Community*. Madison: University of Wisconsin Press.

Hannan, Michael and John Freeman (1977). The Population Ecology of Organizations. *American Journal of Sociology, 82*, 929–64.

Harl, Neil E. (1982). *Delivery of Legal Services in Rural Areas*. Address (mimeographed) given at a colloquium on the delivery of legal services in rural areas, sponsored by the American Bar Association, October 9, Des Moines, Iowa.

Hawley, Amos H. (1950). *Human Ecology: A Theory of Community Structure*. New York: Ronald Press.

——— (1986). *Human Ecology: A Theoretical Essay*. Chicago: University of Chicago Press.

Hazard, Geoffrey C., Jr. (1965). Reflections on Four Studies of the Legal Profession. *Social Problems, 13*, 47–54.

Heinz, John P. and Edward O. Laumann (1982). *Chicago Lawyers: The Social Structure of the Bar*. New York: Russell Sage Foundation; Chicago: American Bar Foundation.

Henderson, Dan Fenno (1982). Law and Political Modernization in Japan. In Robert Ward (ed.), *Political Development in Modern Japan*. Princeton, N.J.: Princeton University Press.

Homans, George (1950). *The Human Group*. New York: Harcourt, Brace, and World.

Hourani, Benjamin T. (1969). The Ecology of Legal Practice and Political Participation. *Journal of Legal Education, 22*, 146–69.

Hughes, Everett C. (1958). *Men and Their Work*. Glencoe, Ill.: Free Press.

Huntin, Roger B. and Gloria Neuwirth. (1962). *Who Sues in New York City? A Study of Automobile Accident Claims*. New York: Columbia University Press.

Hurst, James W. (1950). *The Growth of American Law: The Law Makers*. Boston: Little, Brown.

——— (1981). The Functions of the Courts in the U.S.: 1950–1980. *Law and Society Review, 15*, 401–22.

Jewett, W.L.O. (1898). Early Bar of Northeast Missouri. In A.J.D. Stewart (ed.), *History of the Bench and Bar in Missouri*.

Kasarda, John D. (1974). The Structural Implications of Social System Size: A Three Level Analysis. *American Sociological Review, 39*, 19–28.

Kasarda, John D. and Morris Janowitz (1974). Community Attachment in Mass Society. *American Sociological Review, 39,* 335.

Kidder, Robert L. (1974). Formal Litigation and Professional Insecurity: Legal Entrepreneurship in South India. *Law and Society Review, 9,* 11–31.

Korte, Charles (1980). Urban–Non-Urban Differences in Social Behavior and Social Psychological Models of Urban Impact. *Journal of Social Issues, 36,* 29.

Ladd, Everett Carll, Jr. (1969). *Ideology in America: Change and Response in a City, a Suburb and a Small Town.* Ithaca: Cornell University Press.

Ladinsky, Jack (1963). Careers of Lawyers, Law Practice, and Legal Institutions. *American Sociological Review, 28,* 47–54.

Landon, Donald D. (1982). Lawyers and Localities: The Interaction of Community Context and Professionalism. *American Bar Foundation Research Journal,* 459.

——— (1985). Clients, Colleagues, and Community: The Shaping of Zealous Advocacy in Country Law Practice. *American Bar Foundation Research Journal,* 81–111.

——— (1988). LaSalle Street and Main Street: The Role of Context in Structuring Law Practice. *Law and Society Review, 22,* 2, 213–36.

Larson, Olaf F. (1978). Values and Beliefs of Rural People. In Thomas R. Ford (ed.), *Rural U.S.A.: Persistence and Change.* Ames: Iowa State University Press.

Laumann, Edward O. and John P. Heinz (1977). Specialization and Prestige in the Legal Profession: The Structure of Deference. *American Bar Foundation Research Journal,* 155–216.

——— (1979). The Organization of Lawyers' Work: Size, Intensity, and Co-practice of the Fields of Law. *American Bar Foundation Research Journal,* 217–46.

Laumann, Edward O., Peter V. Marsden, and Joseph Galaskiewicz (1977). Community-elite Influence Structures: Extension of a Network Approach. *American Journal of Sociology, 83,* 598–600.

Lingeman, Richard (1980). *Small Town in America: A Narrative History, 1620 to the Present.* New York: G. P. Putnam's Sons.

Llewellyn, Karl N. (1933). The Bar Specializes—With What Results? *Annals of American Academy of Social and Political Sciences,* 177.

——— (1938). The Bar's Troubles, Poultices—And Cures? *Law and Contemporary Problems, 5,* 1.

Lortie, Dan C. (1958). The Striving Young Lawyer: A Study of Early Career Differentiation in the Chicago Bar. Unpublished Ph.D. dissertation, Sociology Department, University of Chicago.

——— (1959). Laymen to Lawmen: Law School, Careers, and Professional Socialization. *Harvard Education Review, 29,* 352.

——— (1960). *Institutional and Entrepreneurial Careers in Law and Medicine.* Unpublished paper (mimeographed) delivered at the Graduate School of Education, Harvard University.

Lyford, Joseph (1965). *The Talk in Vandalia.* New York: Harper and Row.

Macaulay, Stewart (1963). Non-contractual Relations in Business: A Preliminary Study. *American Sociological Review, 28,* 55.

Martindale, Don and R. Galen Hansen (1969). *Small Town and the Nation: The Conflict of Local and Translocal Forces.* Westport, Conn.: Greenwood Publishing.

Maru, Olavi (1986). *Research in the Legal Profession,* 2nd edition. Chicago: American Bar Foundation.

Matthews, Thomas J. (1952). *The Lawyer as Community Leader: One Dimension of a Professional Role*. Unpublished Ph.D. dissertation, Cornell University.
Mayhew, Leon and Albert J. Reiss, Jr. (1969). The Social Organization of Legal Contacts. *American Sociological Review, 34*, 309–18.
Melone, Albert P. (1972). *Lawyers and the Republic: The ABA and Public Policy*. Unpublished Ph.D. dissertation, University of Iowa.
——— (1980). Rejection of the Lawyer-dominance Proposition: The Need for Additional Research. *Western Political Quarterly, 33*, 225–32.
Merton, Robert (1957). *Social Theory and Social Structure*. Glencoe, Ill.: Free Press.
Miller, Richard E. and Austin Sarat (1980). Grievances, Claims, and Disputes: Assessing the Adversary Culture. *Law and Society Review*, 525.
Mills, C. Wright (1951). *White Collar: The American Middle Classes*. New York: Oxford University Press.
Moon, Charles M., Jr. (1977). *Careers of Lawyers in Politics: The Case of the Georgia General Assembly*. Unpublished Ph.D. dissertation, Georgia State University.
Neef, Marian and Stuart Nagel (1974). The Adversary Nature of the American Legal System from a Historical Perspective. *New York Law Review, 20*, 123.
Nelson, Robert (1983). *Practice and Privilege: The Social Organization of Large Law Firms*. Unpublished dissertation, Northwestern University.
Ogburn, W. F. and Otis D. Duncan (1964). City Size as a Sociological Variable. In Earnest W. Burgess and Donald J. Bogue (eds.), *Contributions to Urban Sociology*. Chicago: University of Chicago Press.
Parsons, Talcott (1951). *The Social System*. Glencoe, Ill.: Free Press.
——— (1954). A Sociologist Looks at the Legal Profession. In Talcott Parsons, *Essays in Sociological Theory*. Glencoe, Ill.: Free Press.
Perrucci, Robert and Joel Gerstl (1969). *Profession without Community*. New York: Random House.
Plumlee, John P. (1981). Lawyers as Bureaucrats: The Impact of Legal Training in the Higher Civil Service. *Public Administration Review, 41*, 220–28.
Pollitt, Daniel H. (1964a). Timid Lawyers and Neglected Clients. *Harpers Magazine*, August, 81–86.
——— (1964b). Counsel for the Unpopular Case: The Hazard of Being Undone. *North Carolina Law Review, 43*, 1.
Pound, Roscoe (1963). *The Causes of Popular Dissatisfaction with the Administration of Justice*. Chicago: American Judicature Society.
Richards, Robert O. (1978). An Examination of Urbanization, Social Organization, and Metropolitan Politics. In David Street et al., *Handbook of Contemporary Urban Life*. San Francisco: Jossey-Bass.
Rubin, J. (1970). Growth and Expansion of Urban Centers. In A. M. Wakstein (ed.), *The Urbanization of America: An Historical Anthology*. Boston: Houghton Mifflin.
Ruchelman, Leonard I. (1966). Lawyers in the New York State Legislature: The Urban Factor. *Midwest Journal of Politcal Science, 10*, 484–97.
Rueschemeyer, Dietrich (1964). Lawyers and Doctors: A Comment on the Theory of Professions. *Canadian Review of Sociology and Anthropology*, 17–30.
——— (1973). *Lawyers and Their Society: A Comparative Study of the Legal Profession in Germany and in the United States*. Cambridge, Mass.: Harvard University Press.

Sarat, Austin (1976). Alternatives in Dispute Processing: Litigation in Small Claims Court. *Law and Society Review, 10,* 339.

Schlesinger, Joseph A. (1957). Lawyers and Politics: A Clarified View. *Midwest Journal of Political Science, 1,* 26–39.

Shils, Edward (1968). Deference. In J. A. Jackson (ed.), *Social Stratification*. Cambridge, England: Cambridge University Press.

Simon, William A. (1978). The Ideology of Advocacy: Procedural Justice and Professional Ethics. *Wisconsin Law Review, 29,* 20.

Smigel, Erwin O. (1969). *The Wall Street Lawyer*. New York: Free Press.

Strick, Anne (1977). *Injustice for All*. New York: G. P. Putnam's Sons.

Taylor, Lee and Arthur R. Jones, Jr. (1964). *Rural Life and Urbanized Society*. New York: Oxford University Press.

Thomas, Edwin J. (1966). Role Conceptions, Organizational Size, and Community Context. In Bruce J. Biddle and Edwin J. Thomas (eds.), *Role Theory: Concepts and Research*. New York: John Wiley and Sons.

Tocqueville, Alexis de (1966). *Democracy in America*. Translated by Henry Reeve. New Rochelle, N.Y.: Arlington House.

Van Es, J. C. and J. E. Brown (1974). The Rural–Urban Variable Once More: Some Individual Level Observations. *Rural Sociology, 39,* 380–81.

Van Velson, J. (1966). Procedural Informality, Reconciliation, and False Comparisons. In Max Gluckman (ed.), *Ideas and Procedures in African Customary Law*. London: Oxford University Press.

Vidich, Arthur J. and Joseph Bensman (1968). *Small Town in Mass Society: Class, Power, and Religion in Rural Community,* revised edition. Princeton, N.J.: Princeton University Press.

Wardwell, Walter I. and Arthur L. Wood (1956). The Extra-professional Role of the Lawyer. *American Journal of Sociology, 61,* 304–7.

Wells, Richard S. (1964). The Legal Profession and Politics. *Midwest Journal of Political Science, 8,* 166–90.

——— (1970). Lawyers and the Allocation of Justice. P. 158 in James R. Klonoski and Robert I. Mendelsohn, *The Politics of Local Justice*. Boston: Little, Brown.

Williams, James (1906). *An American Town*. New York: James Kempster.

Williams, Robin M. (1970). *American Society: A Sociological Interpretation*. New York: Alfred A. Knopf.

Winsborough, Hal H. (1960). Occupational Composition and Urban Hierarchy. *American Sociological Review,* 894–97.

Wolf, Kurt H., trans. and ed. (1950). *The Sociology of Georg Simmel*. New York: The Free Press.

Wood, Arthur L. and Walter Wardwell (1956). The Lawyer and Community Leadership. *Journal of Legal Education, 9,* 162.

Zemans, Frances K. (1982). Framework for Analysis of Legal Mobilization: A Decision-making Model. *American Bar Foundation Research Journal,* 989–1023.

Zemans, Frances K. and Victor Rosenblum (1981). *The Making of a Public Profession*. Chicago: American Bar Foundation.

INDEX

ABOUT THE AUTHOR

DONALD D. LANDON was born May 23, 1930, in Council Bluffs, Iowa, where he graduated from Abraham Lincoln High School in 1948. He received an A.A. degree from Graceland College in Lamoni, Iowa, in 1950, and attended the University of Iowa from 1950 to 1951. From 1951 through 1970, Dr. Landon served in a variety of denominational positions for the Reorganized Church of Jesus Christ of Latter Day Saints, including work in Scandinavia. He concluded his career with the church serving as denominational Commissioner of Education.

Dr. Landon's education includes a B.A. degree in Sociology from the University of Kansas City, an M.A. from the University of Missouri at Kansas City, and the Ph.D. from the University of Kansas. He held a visiting Professorship at Graceland College for a year. In 1970 he joined the Sociology faculty at Southwest Missouri State University in Springfield. He became Head of the Department of Sociology, Anthropology, and Social Work in 1984.

From 1982 to 1983, Dr. Landon served as Visiting Scholar at the American Bar Foundation. During that year he collected the data that forms the basis for the book *Country Lawyers*. The research was done in the state of Missouri, where he personally interviewed nearly 300 practicing lawyers in small towns and a middle-size city (Springfield). He has published papers in leading law and society journals and teaches Sociology of Law at Southwest Missouri State University.

www.ingramcontent.com/pod-product-compliance
Ingram Content Group UK Ltd.
Pitfield, Milton Keynes, MK11 3LW, UK
UKHW021907150926
475560UK00003B/224